More Praise for *Scrum: The Art of Doing Twice the Work in Half the Time*

"This extraordinary book shows a new way to simplify your life and work, increase your focus, and get more done in less time than you ever thought possible."

—Brian Tracy, bestselling author of *Eat That Frog!* and *Time Power*

"Groundbreaking . . . Will upend people's assumptions about how productive they can actually be. . . ." Jeff Sutherland discloses to the non-tech world the elegantly simple process that programmers and web developers have been using since he invented Scrum, showing how a small, empowered, and dedicated team can deliver significantly higher quality work at a faster pace through introspection, iteration, and adaptation."

—Michael Mangi, senior VP of interactive technology,
Social@Ogilvy

"Jeff Sutherland has written the essence of Scrum for the masses. This book elevates Scrum from a fix-it tool to a way of life."

—Hirotaka Takeuchi, professor of management practice,
Harvard Business School

"Jeff Sutherland is *the* master of creating high-performing teams. The subtitle of this book understates Scrum's impact. If you don't get three times the results in one-third the time, you aren't doing it right!"

—Scott Maxwell, founder and senior managing director,
OpenView Venture Partners

"Jeff Sutherland used the common-sense but seldom-applied principles of the quality movement, user-centered design, and lean development to come up with a process that dramatically increases productivity while reducing employees' frustrations with the typical corporate nonsense. **This book is the best description I've seen of how this process can work across many industries.**"

—Jeffrey Pfeffer, professor, Stanford Business School
and co-author of *The Knowing-Doing Gap*

"Sutherland's secret to surmounting professional and personal obstacles is approaching tasks with deliberate attention and a resilient mindset. **This book will change the way you do** *everything*. **Even better, it will help you feel good in the process. Just read it, and get more done.**"

—Arnold V. Strong, CEO of BrightNeighbor.com,
and colonel, US Army Reserve

"This deceptively simple system is the most powerful way I've seen to improve the effectiveness of any team."

—Leo Babauta, creator of Zen Habits

SCRUM

THE ART OF DOING

TWICE THE WORK IN

HALF THE TIME

**Jeff Sutherland
and J. J. Sutherland**

CURRENCY
NEW YORK

Published in the United States by Currency, an imprint of the Crown Publishing Group, a division of Penguin Random House LLC, New York.
crownpublishing.com

CURRENCY and its colophon are trademarks of Penguin Random House LLC.

Originally published in the United States by Crown Business, an imprint of the Crown Publishing Group, a division of Penguin Random House LLC, in 2014.

Currency books are available at special discounts for bulk purchases for sales promotions or corporate use. Special editions, including personalized covers, excerpts of existing books, or books with corporate logos, can be created in large quantities for special needs. For more information, contact Premium Sales at (212) 572-2232 or e-mail specialmarkets@penguinrandomhouse.com.

Library of Congress Cataloging-in-Publication Data is available upon request.

ISBN 978-0-385-34645-0
Ebook ISBN 978-0-385-34646-7

Printed in Canada

Jacket design by Justin Thomas Kay

Photograph on page 206 © Willy Wijnands

16

First Edition

CONTENTS

Preface

Why Scrum?

I first created Scrum, with Ken Schwaber, twenty years ago, as a faster, more reliable, more effective way to create software in the tech industry. Up to that point—and even as late as 2005—most software development projects were created using the Waterfall method, where a project was completed in distinct stages and moved step by step toward ultimate release to consumers or software users. The process was slow, unpredictable, and often never resulted in a product that people wanted or would pay to buy. Delays of months or even years were endemic to the process. The early step-by-step plans, laid out in comforting detail in Gantt charts, reassured management that we were in control of the development process—but almost without fail, we would fall quickly behind schedule and disastrously over budget.

To overcome those faults, in 1993 I invented a new way of doing things: Scrum. It is a radical change from the prescriptive, top-down project management methodologies of the past. Scrum, instead, is akin to evolutionary, adaptive, and self-correcting systems. Since its inception, the Scrum framework has become *the* way the tech industry creates new software and products. But while Scrum has become famously successful in managing software and hardware projects in Silicon Valley, it remains relatively unknown in general business practice. And that is why I wrote *Scrum*:

to reveal and explain the Scrum management system to businesses outside the world of technology. In the book I talk about the origins of Scrum in the Toyota Production System and the OODA loop of combat aviation. I discuss how we organize projects around small teams—and why that is such an effective way to work. I explain how we prioritize projects, how we set up one-week to one-month "sprints" to gain momentum and hold everyone on the team accountable, how we conduct brief daily stand-ups to keep tabs on what has been done and on the challenges that have inevitably cropped up. And how Scrum incorporates the concepts of continuous improvement and minimum viable products to get immediate feedback from consumers, rather than waiting until a project is finished. As you'll see in the pages that follow, we've used Scrum to build everything from affordable 100-mile-per-gallon cars to bringing the FBI database systems into the twenty-first century.

Read on. I think you'll see how Scrum can help transform how your company works, creates, plans, and thinks. I firmly believe that Scrum can help to revolutionize how business works in virtually every industry, just as it has revolutionized innovation and speed to market at a dazzling array of new companies and a breathtaking range of new products emerging out of Silicon Valley and the world of technology.

—Jeff Sutherland, PhD

CHAPTER ONE

The Way the World Works Is Broken

Jeff Johnson was pretty sure it wasn't going to be a good day. On March 3, 2010, the Federal Bureau of Investigation killed its biggest and most ambitious modernization project—the one that was supposed to prevent another 9/11 but that had devolved into one of the biggest software debacles of all time. For more than a decade the FBI had been trying to update its computer system, and it looked as if they would fail. *Again.* And now it was his baby.

He'd shown up at the FBI seven months earlier, lured there by the new Chief Information Officer, Chad Fulgham, whom he'd worked with at Lehman Brothers. Jeff was Assistant Director of the IT Engineering Division. He had an office on the top floor of the J. Edgar Hoover Building in downtown Washington, D.C. It was a big office. It even had a view of the Washington Monument. Little did Jeff know he'd end up in a windowless cinder-block office in the basement for much of the next two years, trying to fix something that everyone believed to be unfixable.

"It was not an easy decision," Jeff says. He and his boss had decided to declare defeat and kill a program that had already taken nearly a decade and cost hundreds of millions of dollars. By that point, it made more sense to bring the project in-house and do it themselves. "But it needed to be done and done well."

The project was the long-awaited computer system that would bring the FBI into the modern age. In 2010—the era of Facebook, Twitter, Amazon, and Google—the FBI was still filing most of its reports on paper. The system the Bureau used was called the Automated Case Support system. It ran on gigantic mainframe computers that had been state of the art sometime in the eighties. Many special agents didn't even use it. It was just too cumbersome and too slow in an era of terror attacks and swift-moving criminals.

When an FBI agent wanted to do something—*anything, really*—from paying an informant to pursuing a terrorist to filing a report on a bank robber, the process wasn't that different from what it had been thirty years earlier. Johnson describes it this way: "You would write up a document in a word processor and print out three copies. One would be sent up the approval chain. One would be stored locally in case that one got lost. And with the third you'd take a red pen—I'm not kidding, a red pen—and circle the key words for input into the database. You'd index your own report."

When a request was approved, that paper copy would drift down from upstairs with a number on it. A number written on a piece of paper is how the FBI kept track of all its case files. This method was so antiquated and porous that it was blamed in part for the Bureau's failure to "connect the dots" that showed various Al Qaeda activists entering the country in the weeks and months before 9/11. One office was suspicious of one person. Another wondered why so many suspicious foreigners were getting flight training. Another had someone on a watch list but never told anyone else. No one in the Bureau ever put it all together.

The 9/11 Commission drilled down after the attack and tried to discover the core reason it was allowed to happen. Analysts, said the Commission, couldn't get access to the very information they were supposed to analyze. "The poor state of the FBI's information systems," reads the report, "meant that such access depended in large part on an analyst's personal relationships with individuals in the operational units or squads where the information resided."

Before 9/11, the FBI had never completed an assessment of the overall terrorism threat to the United States. There were a lot of reasons for this, from focus on career advancement to a lack of information sharing. But the report singled out lack of technological sophistication as perhaps the key reason the Bureau failed so dramatically in the days leading up to 9/11. "The FBI's information systems were woefully inadequate," the Commission's report concludes. "The FBI lacked the ability to know what it knew: there was no effective mechanism for capturing or sharing its institutional knowledge."

When senators started asking the Bureau some uncomfortable questions, the FBI basically said, "Don't worry, we have a modernization plan already in the works." The plan was called the Virtual Case File (VCF) system, and it was supposed to change everything. Not letting any crisis go to waste, officials said they only needed another $70 million on top of the $100 million already budgeted for the plan. If you go back and read press reports on VCF at the time, you'll notice that the words *revolutionary* and *transformation* are used liberally.

Three years later, the program was killed. It didn't work. Not even a little bit. The FBI had spent $170 million in taxpayer money to buy a computer system that would never be used—not a single line of code, or application, or mouse click. The whole thing was an unmitigated disaster. And this wasn't simply IBM or Microsoft making a mistake. People's *lives* were, quite literally, on the line. As Senator Patrick Leahy of Vermont, then the ranking Democrat on the Senate Judiciary Committee, told the *Washington Post* at the time:

> We had information that could have stopped 9/11. It was sitting there and was not acted upon. . . . I haven't seen them correct the problems. . . . We might be in the 22nd century before we get the 21st-century technology.[1]

It is rather telling that many of the people who were at the FBI when the Virtual Case File disaster happened aren't there anymore.

In 2005 the FBI announced a new program, Sentinel. This time it would work. This time they'd put in the right safeguards, the right budget procedures, the right controls. They'd learned their lesson. The price tag? A mere $451 million. And it would be fully operational by 2009.

What could possibly go wrong? In March of 2010 the answer landed on Jeff Johnson's desk. Lockheed Martin, the contractor hired to make the Sentinel system, had already spent $405 million. They'd developed only half of the project, and it was already a year late. An independent analysis estimated it would take another six to eight years to finish the project, and the taxpayers would have to throw in at least another $350 million.

Finding some way around that was Johnson's problem.

What went wrong and how the situation got fixed are why I'm writing this book. It wasn't that these weren't smart people. It wasn't that the Bureau didn't have the right personnel in place, or even the right technology. It wasn't about a work ethic or the right supply of competitive juices.

It was because of the *way* people were working. The way *most* people work. The way we all think work *has* to be done, because that's the way we were taught to do it.

When you hear what happened, it *sounds* at first as if it makes sense: the people at Lockheed sat down before they bid on the contract, looked at the requirements, and started planning how to build a system that would do all that. They had lots of intelligent people working for months, figuring out what needed to be done. Then they spent more months planning how to do it. They produced beautiful charts with everything that needed to be accomplished and the time it would take to complete each and every task. Then, with careful color selection, they showed each piece of the project cascading down to the next like a waterfall.

WATERFALL METHOD

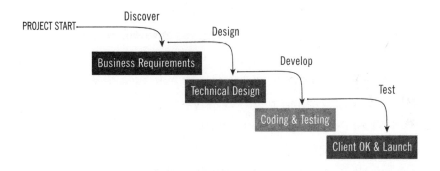

These charts are called Gantt charts, after Henry Gantt, who developed them. With the advent of personal computers in the 1980s making it easy to create these intricate charts—and to make them really *complex*—they have become works of art. Every single step in a project is laid out in detail. Every milestone. Every delivery date. These charts truly are impressive to behold. The only problem with them is that they are always, always *wrong*.

Henry Gantt invented his famous charts around 1910. They were first used in World War I by General William Crozier, who was the Chief of Ordnance for the US Army. Anyone who has studied that war knows that efficient organizational capability was not exactly a salient feature. Why a World War I artifact has become the de facto tool used in twenty-first-century project management has never been quite clear to me. We gave up on trench warfare, but somehow the ideas that organized it are still popular.

It's just so tempting: all the work needed to be done on a massive project laid out for everyone to see. I've visited many companies that have people whose *only job* is to update that Gantt chart every day. The trouble is, once that beautifully elegant plan meets reality, it falls apart. But instead of scrapping the plan, or the way they think about the plan, managers instead hire people to make it look as if the plan is working. Essentially, they're paying people to lie to them.

This unfortunate pattern echoes those reports the Soviet politburo was getting in the 1980s just before the total collapse of the USSR. A complete mirage. Now as then, the reports become more important than the reality they're supposed to describe, and if there's a discrepancy, reality is the problem, not the charts.

When I was a West Point cadet, I slept in Dwight Eisenhower's old room. At night, the streetlights would reflect off a gold plate on the mantelpiece and sometimes wake me up. DWIGHT D. EISENHOWER SLEPT HERE, the plate read. And I'd remember that Eisenhower once observed that planning for combat is important, but as soon as the first shot is fired, your plans go up in smoke. At least he had enough sense not to use a Gantt chart.

So Lockheed presented the FBI with all these lovely charts, and the Bureau signed on. Supposedly, the task was now so well planned out that nothing could go wrong. "Look, it's in the color-coded, time-stamped, bar-graphed plan."

Yet when Jeff and his boss, CIO Chief Chad Fulgham, looked

at the plan in the spring of 2010, they knew it for what it was, what such charts *all* are, really: a complete fabrication. When the two men started to look at actual development and actual deliverables, they realized the problem was beyond fixing. New defects in the software were being discovered faster than old ones were being fixed.

Chad told the Department of Justice Inspector General that they could complete the Sentinel project by bringing development in-house, cutting the number of developers, and that, by doing so, they'd deliver the most challenging half of the project in less than a fifth of the time with less than a tenth of the amount budgeted. The skepticism in the usually dry IG reports to Congress is palpable. In the October 2010 report, after laying out their nine points of concern with the proposal, the IG watchdogs conclude: "In sum, we have significant concerns and questions about the ability of this new approach to complete the Sentinel project within budget, in a timely fashion, and with similar functionality. . . ."[2]

A New Way of Thinking

This new approach is called "Scrum." I created it twenty years ago. Now it is the *only* way proven to help projects like these. There are two ways of doing things: the old "Waterfall" method that wastes hundreds of millions of dollars and often doesn't deliver anything, or the new way, which, with fewer people and in less time, can deliver more stuff with higher quality at lower cost. I know it sounds too good to be true, but the proof is in the results. It works.

Two decades ago I was desperate. I needed a new way of thinking about work. And through tons of research and experimentation and looking over past data I realized we all needed a new way of organizing human endeavor. None of it is rocket science; it's all been talked about before. There are studies going back to World War II that lay out some of the better ways that people work. But for some reason people never really put together all the pieces. Over the past two decades I've tried to do just that, and now this methodology has become ubiquitous in the first field I applied it to, software development. At giants such as Google, Amazon, and Salesforce.com, and at small start-ups you haven't heard of yet, this framework has radically shifted how people get things done.

The reason this framework works is simple. I looked at how people *actually* work, rather than how they *say* they work. I looked at research done over decades and at best practices in companies all over the world, and I looked deeply at the best teams within those companies. What made them superior? What made them different? Why do some teams achieve greatness and others mediocrity?

For reasons I'll get into further in future chapters, I called this framework for team performance "Scrum." The term comes from the game of rugby, and it refers to the way a team works together to move the ball down the field. Careful alignment, unity of purpose, and clarity of goal come together. It's the perfect metaphor for what I want teams to do.

Traditionally, management wants two things on any project: control and predictability. This leads to vast numbers of documents and graphs and charts, just like at Lockheed. Months of effort go into planning every detail, so there will be no mistakes, no cost overruns, and things will be delivered on schedule.

The problem is that the rosy scenario never actually unfolds. All that effort poured into planning, trying to restrict change, trying to know the unknowable is wasted. Every project involves discovery of problems and bursts of inspiration. Trying to restrict a human endeavor of any scope to color-coded charts and graphs is foolish and doomed to failure. It's not how people work, and it's not how projects progress. It's not how ideas reach fruition or how great things are made.

Instead, it leads to frustrated people not getting what they want. Projects are delayed, come in over budget, and, in too many cases, end in abject failure. This is especially true for teams involved in the creative work of crafting something new. Most of the time, management won't learn of the glide path toward failure until millions of dollars and thousands of hours have been invested for naught.

Scrum asks why it takes so long and so much effort to do stuff, and why we're so bad at figuring out how long and how much effort things will take. The cathedral at Chartres took fifty-seven years to build. It's a safe bet that at the beginning of the project the stonemasons looked at the bishop and said, "Twenty years, max. Probably be done in fifteen."

Scrum embraces uncertainty and creativity. It places a structure around the learning process, enabling teams to assess both what they've created and, just as important, how they created it. The Scrum framework harnesses how teams actually work and gives them the tools to self-organize and rapidly improve both speed and quality of work.

At its root, Scrum is based on a simple idea: whenever you start a project, why not regularly check in, see if what you're doing is heading in the right direction, and if it's actually what people want? And question whether there are any ways to improve how you're doing what you're doing, any ways of doing it better and faster, and what might be keeping you from doing that.

That's what's called an "Inspect and Adapt" cycle. Every little while, stop doing what you're doing, review what you've done, and see if it's still what you should be doing and how you might do it better. It's a simple idea, but executing it requires thought, introspection, honesty, and discipline. I'm writing this book to show you how to do it. And not just in software companies. I've seen Scrum used successfully to build cars, run a laundry, teach students in a classroom, make rocket ships, plan a wedding—even, as my wife has used it, to make sure that the "honey-do" list gets done every weekend.

The end results of Scrum—the design goal, if you will—are teams that dramatically improve their productivity. Over the past twenty years I've built these teams over and over and over again. I've been the CEO, CTO, or head of engineering of a dozen companies, from small start-ups with a few people in one room to large enterprises with offices spread across the planet. I've consulted and coached hundreds more.

The results can be so dramatic that leading research and analysis firms such as Gartner, Forrester Research, and the Standish Group now say that the old style of work is obsolete. Companies that still cling to tried-but-not-true ideas of command and control and that attempt to impose rigid predictability are simply doomed to fail if their competitors use Scrum. The difference is too great. Venture capital firms like OpenView Venture Partners in Boston, where I'm an adviser, say that Scrum offers too big a competitive advantage not to use it. These are not warm and fuzzy people; these are gimlet-eyed money men, and they simply say, "The results are indisputable. Companies have two choices: change or die."

Fixing the FBI

At the FBI, the first problem the Sentinel team faced was contracts. Every single change ended up being a contract negotiation with Lockheed Martin. So Jeff Johnson and Chad Fulgham spent months unraveling all the contracts, taking the development inside, and cutting the staff from hundreds to under fifty. The core team was even smaller.

The first week they did what a lot of people in these circumstances do: they printed out all the requirements' documentation. If you've never seen what that looks like on a large project, it can be hundreds and hundreds of pages. I've seen stacks that are several feet high. I've seen this in project after project—people cut and paste and throw in boilerplate, but no one actually reads all those thousands of pages. They can't. That's the point. They've set up a system that forces them to endorse a fantasy.

"There were 1,100 requirements. The stack was a few inches thick," says Johnson. Just thinking about those documents makes me feel for the people who had probably spent weeks of their lives producing those documents that *had no purpose*. The FBI and Lockheed Martin aren't alone in this—I've seen this duplicated at almost every company I have worked with. That tall stack of futility is one of the reasons Scrum can be such a powerful change for people. No one should spend their lives on meaningless work. Not only is it not good business, it kills the soul.

So after they had this stack, they went through and prioritized each requirement. Which is vitally important and trickier than it sounds. Often people simply say that everything is important. But what they need to ask, what the Sentinel teams asked, was, what will bring the most *value* to the project? Do those things first. In software development there is a rule, borne out by decades of research, that 80 percent of the value in any piece of software is in 20 percent of the features. Think about it: when was the last time you used the Visual Basic Editor function in Microsoft Word? You probably don't know what Visual Basic is, let alone why you'd use it. But it's there, and someone spent time implementing it, but I guarantee you, it doesn't increase the value of Word by much.

Making people prioritize by value forces them to produce that 20 percent first. Often by the time they're done, they realize they don't really need the other 80 percent, or that what seemed important at the outset actually isn't.

For the Sentinel team, the question became, "Okay, we're doing this huge project that is vitally important that we've wasted hundreds of millions of dollars on. When will it be done?" After thinking on it, they promised delivery in the fall of 2011. The Inspector General report from the fall of 2010 is a study in disbelief:

> The FBI stated that it will employ an "agile methodology" to complete the development of Sentinel, using fewer employees from the FBI, Lockheed Martin, and the companies that have supplied the major off-the-shelf components of Sentinel. Overall the FBI plans to reduce the number of contract employees working on Sentinel from approximately 220 to 40. The FBI said that, at the same time, the number of FBI employees assigned to the project will also decrease from 30 to 12. . . . The FBI told us it believes it can complete Sentinel with the approximately $20 million remaining in the Sentinel budget and within 12 months of beginning this new approach.[3]

The use of the phrase "agile methodology" shows just how little the IG knew about Scrum. The term "Agile" dates back to a

2001 conclave where I and sixteen other leaders in software development wrote up what has become known as the "Agile Manifesto." It declared the following values: people over processes; products that actually work over documenting what that product is supposed to do; collaborating with customers over negotiating with them; and responding to change over following a plan. Scrum is the framework I built to put those values into practice. There is no methodology.

Of course Johnson's twelve-month promise was somewhat misleading. Because, in actuality, they didn't know; they couldn't know. The FBI didn't know how fast their teams could actually work. It's something I tell executives all the time: "I'll know what the date will be when I see how much the teams improve. How fast they'll get. How much they'll *accelerate*."

It was also crucial, of course, that team members figure out what would *stop* them from accelerating. As Jeff Johnson put it, "I handled impediment removal." An "impediment" is an idea that comes from the company that first formed a lot of the ideas Scrum is based on: Toyota. And, more specifically, Taiichi Ohno's Toyota Production System.

I won't go into all the details here, but one of the key concepts that Ohno introduced is the idea of "flow." That is, production should flow swiftly and calmly throughout the process, and, he said, one of management's key tasks is to identify and remove impediments to that flow. Everything that stands in the way is waste. Ohno gives waste a moral, as well as a business, value in his classic book, *The Toyota Production System*:

> It is not an exaggeration that in a low-growth period such waste is a crime against society more than a business loss. Eliminating waste must be a business's first objective.[4]

Ohno talks a lot about the different kinds of waste and impediments that can get in the way of production. For Scrum to really take off, someone in senior management needs to understand in his bones that impediments are nearly criminal. I'll tell you *how* to eliminate waste later on in the book. Suffice it to say here that the effect of eliminating waste is dramatic, but people often don't do it, because it requires being honest with themselves and with others.

Jeff Johnson knew that was his job.

It took the Sentinel team about three months to figure out how long completing the project would *really* take. Why? This goes back to that "Inspect and Adapt" cycle I talked about earlier. Scrum works by setting sequential goals that must be completed in a fixed length of time. In the FBI's case, they decided on two-week cycles, with the understanding that, at the end of each cycle, there would be a *finished* increment of product. That meant they'd have something working, something that could be shown to anyone who cared to look but certainly the stakeholders and, optimally, the people who'd actually be using the thing.

This methodology allows teams to get near real-time feedback on their work. Are they headed in the right direction? Is what they're planning to do next *really* what they should be doing, given what they've discovered during that cycle?

In Scrum we call these cycles "Sprints." At the beginning of each cycle there is a meeting to plan the Sprint. The team decides how much work they think they can accomplish during the next two weeks. They'll take the work items off that prioritized list of things that need to be done and often just write them out on sticky notes and put them on the wall. The team decides how many of those work items they can get done during this Sprint.

At the end of the Sprint, the team comes together and shows

what they've accomplished during the time they've collaborated. They look at how many of those sticky notes they actually got done. Did they bring too many into the Sprint and not finish them all? Did they not bring enough? What's important here is that they begin to have a baseline sense of how fast they can go—their velocity.

After they've shown what they've done—and here's where Ohno's ideas come in—they discuss not what they did, but *how* they did it. They ask, "How can we work together better in the next Sprint? What was getting in our way during the last one? What are the impediments that are slowing our velocity?" You can find a more detailed explanation of how Scrum works in the appendix.

And that's why Jeff Johnson needed a few months before he could really tell how long the project would take. He wanted to measure the velocity of each team measured over a few Sprints and then see how much they could improve—how much faster they could go. Once he looked at how many work items each team had finished in each Sprint and then checked how many they had remaining until the end of the project, he could forecast a completion date.

Besides learning how fast the teams were going, he also wanted to know what impediments were slowing them down. What he really wanted to do was *accelerate* those teams so they were producing faster—not by working longer hours (I'll go into why that's a fruitless rat hole that ends up making things take longer later) but by working *better* and *smarter*. Jeff Johnson says his teams increased their productivity by *a factor of three*. They were going three times as fast once they got moving as compared to when they started. Why? They got better at working together, yes, but most important, they figured out the things that were slowing them down, and each cycle, each Sprint, they'd try to get rid of them.

It eventually took the Sentinel project eighteen months of coding to get the database system deployed, and another two months to deploy it to the entire FBI. "Tremendous time pressure," Johnson said when he sat down for an interview. "And you have to understand, the system is used for *everything*. Paying informants. Storing evidence. Case files. Calendars. This *meeting* is in Sentinel."

And the most powerful part of Scrum from his point of view? "Demos. Driving toward a demonstrable product on a frequent basis." Every two weeks the Sentinel team would demonstrate what they'd accomplished. And this show-and-tell wasn't just to themselves. They were taking what they'd achieved and running it by the people who would actually be using the system. Everyone who had a stake in the project sent someone and that could make for a pretty full house. Records. Intelligence. Special agents. The Office of the Inspector General. Representatives from other government agencies. Often enough, the Director and Deputy Director of the FBI were in the room, as was the acting Inspector General herself. This was *not* an easy crowd.

And that was what made it work, says Johnson. "Scrum is not about the developers. It's about the customers and stakeholders. Really, it was an organizational change. Showing the *actual product* was the most powerful part."

Actually showing the product was powerful, because people were, to put it mildly, skeptical of the team's reported progress. They just couldn't believe Sentinel's progress actually kept moving at a faster and faster rate. "I was saying to Congress that with 5 percent of the budget and in twenty months we were going to accomplish what Lockheed couldn't do with 90 percent of the budget in ten years," says Johnson. "There was skepticism in the room. We had to provide reports to the Associate Attorney General. We would be transparent with our status, but our audience would assume something devious was going on. Anytime they'd seen those kinds of indicators in the past, the reports were less detailed, and something else *was* going on."

And that skepticism infected the rest of the FBI. *The guys down in the basement are just going to screw it up again,* was the thinking. This will just be one more temporary system that will fail, and we'll have to go back to using paper.

Jeff told his team about a passage he had to memorize when he was a Naval cadet at Annapolis. It was from Teddy Roosevelt's speech "Citizenship in a Republic," which he gave at the Sorbonne in 1910. It is oft-quoted, and you may be already familiar with it:

It is not the critic who counts; not the man who points out how the strong man stumbles, or where the doer of deeds could have done them better. The credit belongs to the man who is actually in the arena, whose face is marred by dust and sweat and blood; who strives valiantly; who errs, who comes short again and again, because there is no effort without error and shortcoming; but who does actually strive to do the deeds; who knows great enthusiasms, the great devotions; who spends himself in a worthy cause; who at the best knows in the end the triumph of high achievement, and who at the worst, if he fails, at least fails while daring greatly, so that his place shall never be with those cold and timid souls who neither know victory nor defeat.[5]

The team did have some delays as they figured out exactly how fast they could do things, and just how hard things were to do. Finally in July of 2012, they turned Sentinel on. And they had to turn it on all the way, to everybody, all at once. There was no way to stage it.

"It happened from one day to the next. In a criminal case or a counterterrorism case, something in Los Angeles might be related to something in Chicago," says Jeff Johnson. "We couldn't allow leads to be lost. *At every point we had to have a clean and known good state.*"

And that state had to be clean and good enough to hold up in court. The data in Sentinel was being used to prosecute people, and its integrity had to be beyond a shadow of doubt.

Jeff was frantic and nervous that first day. He went into his office and turned on Sentinel. It loaded. That was a good thing. And then he tried to approve a document with an electronic signature—a basic everyday task that tens of thousands of FBI employees would have to do all the time. Up came an error message. It didn't work. He started to panic, Johnson remembers, visions of disaster dancing in his head. And then he looked carefully at the error code and realized what it meant. He hadn't inserted his ID card into the machine to verify his identity. He put in the card, clicked his mouse, and Sentinel was good to go.

The effect of Sentinel on the FBI has been dramatic. The ability to communicate and share information has fundamentally changed what the Bureau is capable of. In January of 2013 an FBI field office was called in when a small-business account was hacked. A million dollars was transferred to another country before US banks could stop it. Using Sentinel, the local office coordinated with the legal attaché in the destination country's embassy, who then alerted local law enforcement authorities, who, in turn, stopped the transfer before it hit the banking system. This all happened in a matter of hours, something that simply couldn't have been done in the days of three paper copies and red pens. It was the difference between catching a crook and letting him get away with it.

In the basement of the FBI the Sentinel team is still there, the panels removed from their cubicles so they can see one another. There's a poster-size copy of the "Agile" principles on the wall—principles I helped write and have devoted my life to implementing around the world. Amazingly enough for a room without windows, a healthy lavender plant thrives under fluorescent lights as you enter the room. "Lavender" was the code name of the Sentinel prototype. The team members are still at their posts, making improvements and adding new functionality to the system they built.

There's an old joke in the Scrum community. A chicken and a pig are walking down the road, and the chicken says, "Hey, Pig, I was thinking we should open up a restaurant."

"What should we call it?" asks the pig.

"How about 'Ham and Eggs'?"

"No thanks," says the pig. "I'd be committed, but you'd only be involved!"

The idea in Scrum is that the "pigs" are the ones who are totally committed to the project and are responsible for its outcome. The "chickens" are the people who are informed of its progress, the stakeholders. On the wall in the Sentinel room is a pig-shaped bell. When it rings, the people who did what everyone said couldn't be done know they're being called. There's another bell, the doorbell, but that's for the chickens.

The world is constantly getting more complicated, and the work we do is gaining in complexity at an ever-increasing rate. Take cars, for example. I used to work on my car all the time doing basic repairs. Thirty years ago I could rebuild a radiator. Now, when I pop open the hood, I may as well be looking at the insides of a computer. Actually, that's basically what I *am* doing, since a new Ford has more lines of code in it than Facebook and Twitter combined. Creating something that complex is a massive human

endeavor. Whenever people are involved in a complex, creative effort, whether they're trying to send a rocket to space, build a better
light switch, or capture a criminal, traditional management meth-
ods simply break apart.

And we know this—as individuals and as a society. We see
echoes of our real lives captured in fictional workplace dystopias
like those depicted in the cartoon *Dilbert* or the movie *Office Space*.
We've all gone home and told our partners or friends of the madness that is modern corporate "organization." We've all been told
that filling out the form correctly is more important than doing
the work, or that we need to have a meeting to prep for the pre-
meeting meeting. It's madness. And yet we keep on doing it. Even
in the face of absolute and complete failure.

The launch of Healthcare.gov, the website where Americans
are supposed to be able to sign up for health insurance, is a great
example. The front end was beautiful. It was clever, clear—a great
design. It was completed in three months using Scrum. The back
end, though—*that* was the debacle. It simply didn't work. It was
supposed to hook up databases in the IRS to state databases, to
insurance company databases, to the department of Health and
Human Services. This is a complex piece of work. It involved more
than twenty contractors working on different bits and pieces, and
they planned it all using Waterfall techniques. They only tested the
site at the very end for a few days, rather than doing incremental
testing along the way.

The tragedy is that everyone knew better. The people who
work for those contractors aren't stupid; they knew better. The
problem was, everyone said, "Not my job." They delivered their
piece and left it at that. They never looked at the site from the
user's point of view, merely from their own. The reason they could
do that was that they weren't aligned—weren't united in a com-

mon purpose. What Scrum does is bring teams together to create great things, and that requires everyone not only to see the end goal, but to deliver incrementally toward that goal. There was no one in charge of the Healthcare.gov project who insisted everything be tested as it was built, and, unfortunately, as failures go, the site is hardly atypical. The people who fixed Healthcare.gov? They used Scrum.

How many times do you hear about some massive project costing millions and millions being cancelled not only because of the cost overruns, but because it simply *doesn't work*? How many billions of dollars are spent each year producing *nothing*? How much of your life is wasted on work that both you and your boss realize doesn't create value? You might as well be digging holes and filling them in again, for all the impact you're having.

It doesn't have to be this way. It really doesn't. Just because everyone has always told you that's the way the world works doesn't mean they're right. There *is* a different way of doing things—a different way of working.

And if you *don't* do it, you'll be outsourced. Or your company will die. The hypercompetitive world of twenty-first-century work has no room for waste and foolishness.

A further important point: working in a maximally productive way—the Scrum way—doesn't have to be confined to business. What if people used this method to address the big problems our species struggles with—such as dependence on oil, or poor education, or lack of clean water in impoverished parts of the globe, or rampant crime? What if there really was a better way to live and work and solve problems differently? A way we really could change the world? There *is*. There are people using Scrum to address each of those problems I've mentioned, and they're making a powerful impact.

SCRUM

In this book you're going to learn some of the fundamental ways that people work best, why we're awful at estimating, and why working overtime will make your project late. I'm going to take you through all the research and applications that people and scientists and organizations have diligently done for years, and how Scrum ties it all together in a way that you can implement tomorrow.

I'm going to show you *how*. First, though, I want to tell the story of how I got here.

THE TAKEAWAY

Planning Is Useful. Blindly Following Plans Is Stupid. It's just so *tempting* to draw up endless charts. All the work needed to be done on a massive project laid out for everyone to see—but when detailed plans meet reality, they fall apart. Build into your working method the assumption of change, discovery, and new ideas.

Inspect and Adapt. Every little while, stop doing what you're doing, review what you've done, and see if it's still what you should be doing and if you can do it better.

Change or Die. Clinging to the old way of doing things, of command and control and rigid predictability, will bring only failure. In the meantime, the competition that is willing to change will leave you in the dust.

Fail Fast So You Can Fix Early. Corporate culture often puts more weight on forms, procedures, and meetings than on visible value creation that can be inspected at short intervals by users. Work that does not produce real value is madness. Working product in short cycles allows early user feedback and you can *immediately* eliminate what is obviously wasteful effort.

CHAPTER TWO

The Origins of Scrum

For American fighter pilots in Vietnam, a tour of duty meant flying one hundred missions into enemy territory. Fifty percent of the pilots got shot down. Some were rescued, but most never made it back. In 1967, as a young, somewhat wet-behind-the-ears fighter pilot, I was shipped from Mountain Home Air Force Base in Idaho to Udorn Royal Thai Air Force Base in Northern Thailand to do what was the most dangerous job in the US Air Force: reconnaissance.

This was long before the age of Predator drone missions and reliable satellite imagery. My RF-4C Phantom was stripped of all weapons and equipped with cameras and an extra fuel tank. My job was to fly into enemy territory so that my navigator could take before-and-after photos of our bombing missions. Most of the missions were at night, and I'd race through the tropical darkness just a few hundred feet from the ground, almost brushing the treetops. The moment I crossed over the border into North Vietnam, my Heads-Up display would light up like a pinball machine, and the loud missile-warning system would go off with a flurry of beeps and whistles. The sky would brighten with tracer fire from antiaircraft guns, and I knew that, in minutes, missile radar would soon be pinpointing my aircraft unless 500 feet was low enough to stay in the ground clutter.

During these moments my adrenaline would pump, but I never lost my cool. Instead, the danger almost settled me. I credit this to the training I got from the Air Force on how to control risk. That training taught me to do four things: **O**bserve, **O**rient, **De**cide, and **A**ct. Specifically, I would observe the target area, figure out the best path into the hot zone and the best path out, orient myself in the face of unexpected events, and then act decisively based on instincts and hardwiring. Hesitation could get pilots killed, but so did foolhardiness. As soon as my navigator had taken his pictures, I'd yank back on the stick and pull up out of the hot zone, the g-force reducing my vision to a pinprick. My navigator often passed out from the g-force or, in some cases, lost control of his bowels. But he never complained. Because I always got us back alive.

Back then I was just a young jet pilot hoping to survive my required missions. I didn't know that my flight experience, and the training I'd received on how to think and act in a life-or-death situation, would shape the way I would work for the rest of my life. I arrived in Vietnam in 1967 with two squadrons of F-4 fighters and two RF-4C reconnaissance aircraft, one hundred planes in total. The aircraft replaced two squadrons of RF-101s. Of those fifty RF-101s, all but four had been shot down in one year. The four remaining had so many bullet holes, they were unflyable. I'm not sure how their pilots landed them after their last mission. The RF-4C was a more resilient fighter plane, but half of our aircraft were still shot down within a year. We'd improved survivability, but still 50 percent of those who showed up with me didn't make it back to base. The lucky ones were rescued from the jungle before they could be imprisoned.

When I returned from the Vietnam war, I pursued a Master's degree from Stanford in statistics and spent as much time as possible at the Stanford Artificial Intelligence Laboratory. From there I became a professor of mathematics at the Air Force Academy, where I embarked on a PhD program in biometrics at the University of Colorado Medical School. There I asked my adviser, Dr. John Bailar, one of the most distinguished researchers in medicine and statistics, how I could do a thesis that would be useful and not wind up on a dusty shelf in the library. He handed me three hundred medical-journal papers on cancer. Each had graphs showing cancer statistics, which varied wildly for humans and animals and tumor types. Bailar said that if I could explain why they were all different, he'd award me a doctoral degree. So that's what I did, and I got that degree.

How I did it was by spending years trying to figure out what happens in a cell to turn it cancerous. I learned a lot about systems theory and how a system only has certain stable states. As a cell evolves, it moves from one stable state to another. Figuring out the rules to move a complex adaptive system from one state to another, and how to make the next state a positive one rather than a negative one, was something I spent nearly a decade on.

Years later it occurred to me that organizations, teams, and people are all complex adaptive systems. The same things that move cells from one state to another are also what move people from one state to another. To change a cell, you first inject energy into the system. At first there's chaos, there seem to be no rules, everything is in flux. When you do this to organizations trying to change, people often freak out. They can't understand what's happening. They don't know what to do. But remarkably quickly, just like a cell, an organization settles into a new steady state. The only question is whether the new state is better than the old one. Is the cell cancerous or healthy? *How,* I wondered, *can we figure out some simple rules that will guide teams to settle into a more productive, happier, supportive, fun, and ecstatic state?* I spent the next fifteen years trying to figure that out.

During the Reagan administration, the government radically cut grants for scientific research, including my National Cancer Centers research grant, where I was Principal Investigator of data collection and analysis for Colorado Regional Cancer Center clinical trials and epidemiology studies. As I was figuring out what to do, a company called MidContinent Computer Services contacted me because they heard I was the leading expert in the area of their newest technology. MidContinent was in the business of servicing 150 banks across North America. Their hottest new product was what they called an "Automatic Teller Machine" network. This was in 1983, when getting cash usually meant standing in line at the bank or pulling up to the bank's drive-through window in your car. You'd write a check out to "cash" in the amount you wanted and hand it to the teller.

ATMs were going to solve this hassle, but back then MidContinent was having problems getting its networks to talk to one another. They needed someone who'd been thinking about systems to fix this, and they made me a lucrative offer to be a vice president of advanced systems. Their network computers were the same machines I'd spent years running my doctoral programs on, so it was a good fit.

Or so I thought. Nothing is ever easy, is it? When I walked

into the company, I came upon a division doing Waterfall-method projects. There were hundreds of computer programmers who sat at their desks all day ostensibly working, but they couldn't deliver anything on time or on budget. For the Automated Teller Machines, costs were 30 percent higher than revenue. The inefficiencies were mind-boggling.

I spent some time early on trying to figure out how things worked. You can imagine how upper management treated my guys. There was a lot of screaming and micromanaging and passive-aggressive behavior and demands for harder work and overtime. But no matter how much management pressed, the projects were still chronically late, still over budget, and not delivering what they were supposed to.

I decided the best option was for us to change everything. The operation was too broken to fix piecemeal, so I decided to make a company within a company. I asked our CEO, Ron Harris, to let me form a separate organization with everyone who was involved in the ATM networks. We'd have our own sales team, our own marketing team, and our own finance people. Ron was a brilliant and creative CEO who trusted my work. Perhaps under someone else this would never have happened. After hearing my idea, he told me, "Sutherland, if you want that kind of headache, take it."

I did. I went to the developers and managers and told them, "The first thing we need to do is to stop doing stuff that is killing us." It's like that old joke about banging your head against a brick wall just so it feels good when you stop. "We've got to figure out a better way of working," I told them, "and we have to start immediately."

So we ran the entire small company as one team split up into sub-teams. Bonuses weren't based on individual performance; they were based on total company performance. We came up with tools that found their way into Scrum ten years later—for example, the concept of a Product Owner, a Product Backlog, and weekly Sprints, which I'll eventually get into more deeply, and which are laid out in the appendix. In six months, we were the most profitable division in the company. Revenue was 30 percent higher than expenses. Our Nonstop Tandem systems were the first online transaction computers that banks trusted enough to use. We deployed them all over North America. Nowadays just about anywhere you go in the country, you can find an ATM machine. And all those machines know exactly how much money you have. My team had a lot to do with that. And, yes, you're welcome.

Learning to Think Like a Robot

After my first career in the military and my second in academia, I found myself something of an outsider in business. But that outsider's perspective was one of my most valuable assets. From day one, it was a mystery to me why people insist on working in ways they *know* are inefficient and wasteful and that are dehumanizing and depressing. I guess they figure that's the way everyone does it, so it must be the best way.

I really enjoyed my time at MidContinent, but I was eager to test my skills on new challenges. For the next two decades I ended up working for companies large and small as VP of Engineering or Chief Technology Officer. At each, I tried to get teams to work together in more efficient ways. At one of those companies, I found myself in a building in Cambridge, Massachusetts, just a few blocks from MIT. A few PhDs and professors had just started a new company building robots, and they'd run out of room in their lab at MIT. They ended up subletting some office space from my company.

A few weeks after they moved in, the most unexpected thing happened: a six-legged robot, the size of a cat, ran into my office and began chasing me around my desk. The roboticists came in and nervously apologized for their machine, but every few days it would happen again. One of the robots would escape their lab and start running around the building. I'd hear the mechanical clacking of legs scurrying down the hallways.

On Friday afternoons I always served wine and beer at the office so that everyone could unwind and socialize after a hard week. I'd invite the roboticists down the hall to these events, and one Friday afternoon Rodney Brooks showed up. Brooks, a professor of artificial intelligence at MIT, was one of the founders of the robot company. I asked him how the roving robots worked.

"For decades we've tried to make a really smart thinking machine," he told me. "We spent billions of dollars, many, many years of work, building the biggest computers we could, with the biggest databases, but all we got was a computer that can beat people at chess."

His robots, he explained, took a completely different approach. Rather than try to build something with a single central brain, they built a robot in which each of the six legs had its own brain. A processor in the spine had a few simple rules: move forward, go back, don't bump into other legs. The neural-network chip in the head of the robot knew these rules and acted as referee for all the parts. It told the legs what it was seeing through its camera when it hit an obstacle—that kind of thing.

What's interesting, Brooks said, is that each time you turn on the robot, it learns to walk for the first time. There is no database of where everything is in the room. Instead, the world is its database. It figures everything out for the first time each time it is switched on. It bumps into things and figures things out based on the actual surroundings, which means it can adapt to any environment.

"Let me show you," he said as he took me over to their lab. He popped a blank neural chip into one of the insectoid robots, and I watched it wobble to life. Hesitantly at first, it stumbled around the room like a fawn picking itself up on its legs for the first time. With each step it became more and more assured. The legs quickly learned to collaborate and work together. Within a few minutes the robot was racing around the room. Nothing was stored or programmed about how to walk; instead, a few simple rules kept these components working together. These legs didn't think; they just did. I was blown away by the ingenuity and simplicity of the system. Here was something that was doing exactly what I was trained to do flying in Vietnam: **O**bserve, **O**rient, **D**ecide, and **A**ct. It was taking in its environment and behaving decisively based on the data from that environment.

"What would happen," I asked Brooks, "if we could come up with a simple instruction set for teams of people to work together just like those legs? They would self-organize and self-optimize, just like that robot."

"I don't know," he replied. "Why don't you try it and let me know how it works out?"

Don't Go Chasing Waterfalls

More and more I realized that, if I could create a system that, like that robot, could coordinate independent thinkers with constant feedback about their environment, much higher levels of performance would be achieved. By streamlining the flow of information among "legs" of a group, we could achieve efficiencies that had never been reached before.

My conversation with Rodney Brooks took place more than two decades ago. For many years he was the head of robotics and artificial intelligence at MIT, and that spidery robot I met, dubbed "Genghis Khan," now sits in the Smithsonian as a collector's item. By now you're probably familiar with one of Brooks's companies, iRobot, which makes the Roomba vacuum cleaner and uses the same adaptive intelligence to clean your floors that Genghis Khan used to chase me around my office. His latest innovation at Rethink Robotics, the Baxter robot, can work collaboratively with humans in a common workspace.

I was inspired by Brooks's work. And in 1993 I took those ideas with me to a company called Easel, where I was hired as VP of Object Technology. The executives at Easel wanted my team to develop a completely new product line in six months that would be aimed at some of their biggest customers—such as the Ford Motor Company, which used their software to design and build internal applications. I sat down with my development team and told them I knew they couldn't do it using the same old way of developing software.

That old methodology was the Waterfall method I described in the last chapter: everything related to a project carefully laid out on those massive Gantt charts, every task measured out precisely in hours highlighted in pretty colors flowing down the page like a waterfall. Those charts were beautiful in their precision. They were also complete fabrications.

At Easel, I knew the Waterfall methodology would put us months if not years past our deadline. We had to come up with a completely different way of doing things. I went to the CEO and told him we were scrapping the Gantt chart. He was shocked and demanded to know why.

"How many Gantt charts have you seen in your career?" I asked.

"Hundreds," he replied.

"How many of them were right?"

He paused. "None."

That's when I told him I was going to give him working software at the end of the month instead of a broken Gantt chart. He could try it out for himself and see if we were on track. We had to try it, if we were going to meet our deadline.

My team and I spent a few weeks reading hundreds of papers and books and articles on the organization of teams and product development. Then one day, one of the developers came in with a *Harvard Business Review* paper from 1986, written by two Japanese business professors, Hirotaka Takeuchi and Ikujiro Nonaka. It was titled, "The New New Product Development Game." Takeuchi and Nonaka had looked at teams from some of the world's most productive and innovative companies: Honda, Fuji-Xerox, 3M, Hewlett-Packard, and others. They argued that the old way of doing product development, typified by NASA's Phased Program Planning system—a Waterfall system—was fundamentally flawed. Instead, the best companies used an overlapping development process that was faster and more flexible. The teams were cross-functional. The teams had autonomy. They were empowered to make their own decisions. And they had a transcendent purpose. They were reaching for something bigger than themselves. Management didn't dictate. Instead, executives were servant-leaders and facilitators focused on getting obstacles out of their teams' way rather than telling them what and how to do product development. The Japanese professors compared the teams' work to that of a rugby team and said the best teams acted as though they were in a scrum: ". . . the ball gets passed within the team as it moves as a unit up the field."[1]

Takeuchi and Nonaka's paper made a splash when it was first published, but that was seven years before we were reading the paper at Easel. Everyone had admired it, but no one had done anything with it. The average American manager was unable to make sense of it even though Toyota was rapidly increasing market share using this approach. At Easel we had nothing to lose. We decided to try it, even though the paper focused on manufacturing, not software development. I thought their ideas tapped into something fundamental, a descriptive process of how humans work together best in any endeavor. It flowed into all the other experiments I'd conducted, going back to my first job in the private sector at Mid-Continent.

This was the formal birth of "Scrum." We delivered the product at Easel on schedule within six months, under budget, and with fewer bugs than any previous delivery.

I got so excited about the possibilities of this new form of project management that all my future work focused on refining Scrum for companies. In 1995 I presented a paper with Ken Schwaber, called "SCRUM Development Process," which codified those practices at an Association for Computing Machinery research conference. Since then we have dropped the all-caps and tweaked the idea a little bit, but the fundamental principles are the same—and those companies that embrace the process typically see immediate benefits.[2]

Inspect and Adapt

Scrum teams that work well are able to achieve what we call "hyperproductivity." It's hard to believe, but we regularly see somewhere between a 300- to 400-percent improvement in productivity among groups that implement Scrum well. The best teams can achieve productivity increases of up to 800 percent and replicate that success over and over again. They also end up more than doubling the *quality* of their work.

So how do you build autonomy, transcendence, and cross-fertilization into a Scrum team and from that combination achieve hyperproductivity? Well, that's what the rest of this book is about, but I'm going to lay out the basic structure here. You can also see it laid out in short form in the appendix.

Since Scrum comes out of techniques used in Japanese manufacturing, it pays to learn a bit about where the Japanese learned them. Ironically, they learned many from an American: W. Edwards Deming. Deming worked for General Douglas MacArthur during the American occupation of Japan after World War II. MacArthur's approach to rebuilding the economy was to fire most of the senior management in Japanese companies, promote line managers from the ranks, and bring in business operations experts like Deming from the United States. Deming's influence on Japanese manufacturing was dramatic. He trained hundreds of engineers in what is called "statistical process control." The basic idea is to measure exactly what is being done, and how well, and to strive for "continuous improvement." Don't just get better once; get better constantly. Always be looking for something to improve. Never, ever settle for where you are. How you get there is to be constantly creating experiments to see if you can achieve improvement. If I try this method, is it better? How about this one? What if I change just this one thing?

Deming famously gave a talk to Japanese business leaders in 1950. In the audience were people like Akio Morita, the founder of Sony. In that talk Deming told them:

> . . . no matter how excellent your technicians, you who are leaders must strive for advances in the improvement of product quality and uniformity if your technicians are to be able to make improvements. The first step, therefore, belongs with management. First, your company technicians and your factories must know that you have a fervor for advancing product quality and uniformity and a sense of responsibility for product quality.
>
> Nothing will come of this if you only speak about it. Action is important.[3]

And the method to take action, and perhaps what Deming is most famous for, is the PDCA cycle (**P**lan, **D**o, **C**heck, **A**ct). You can apply this cycle to the production of just about anything, be it a car, a videogame, or, heck, even a paper airplane.

When I train people how to do Scrum, that's what I use: paper airplanes. I divide people up into teams and tell them that the goal is to build as many paper airplanes as they can that will fly across the room. There are going to be three roles on the team. One person will check how many planes are built that can actually fly. Another will work as part of the assembly process but will also pay attention to the process itself and look for ways that the team can make better planes and speed up their production. Everyone else will concentrate on building as many planes that can actually fly the distance in the assembly time allowed.

I then say we're going to do three six-minute cycles of paper-airplane building. The teams have one minute each cycle to Plan how they're going to build the airplane, three minutes to Do—to build and test as many airplanes as they can that can actually fly. And finally they'll have two minutes to Check. In this phase the team looks for how they could improve their paper airplane–building process. What went right? What went wrong? Should the design be changed? How can the construction process be improved? And then they will Act. In Deming's world "to act" means to change your way of working based on real results and real environmental input. It's the same strategy used by Brooks's robot.

Go through this cycle three times, and whether you're making paper airplanes or actual spaceships you'll get better—significantly better (on the order of two to three times faster with at least double the quality). This PDCA cycle, a radical idea when Deming pitched it to the Japanese, is how Toyota became the number one car company in the world. And it's how any sort of "Lean" manufacturing (the American term for using the concepts of the Toyota Production System), or Scrum product development, is done.

Change or Die

Part of the reason a new way of doing things was so imperative, and why such a broad swath of companies have adopted it, is because the state of software development was so bad. Projects were almost always late, over budget, and often simply didn't work. And that wasn't because people were stupid or greedy—rather, it had to do with the way they thought about their work. They insisted on the Waterfall method, insisted that everything could be planned ahead of time, even insisted that things *wouldn't change* over the course of a multiyear project. That's just insane on the face of it.

I learned this firsthand at BellSouth, when I visited them as a consultant years ago. They had top-notch engineers, many from the famous Bell Labs. They executed Waterfall perfectly. They'd bid on huge $10- to $20-million projects. They'd gather all the requirements from the customer, then go away for eighteen months and deliver on time and on budget exactly what the customer had asked for. They were one of the very, very few companies in the entire world that could pull that off. The problem was, at that point the customer no longer wanted what they'd said they wanted. Circumstances had changed. Business cycles were getting shorter, and customers were demanding more responsive services.

I was brought in to see if I could help BellSouth figure out what they were doing wrong. I soon realized it was the entire way they were working. This can be tough to hear when it seems as if you're doing everything right. So one day I stood before a roomful of 150 BellSouth engineers and told them that unless they changed to a different, more customer-responsive model, they wouldn't last as a going concern. The crowd was tough. They were all really smart men and women, but they believed my ideas were just another management fad. I couldn't get through to them, so I just shrugged and left them with a final warning: "Change or die." As you may have noticed, BellSouth isn't around anymore.

Shu Ha Ri

Scrum has its roots in Japanese thought and practice. When I travelled to Japan recently to meet with Professor Ikujiro Nonaka, he made it clear to me that in Japan Scrum isn't seen as the latest work fad. They regard it as a way of doing, a way of being, a way of life. When I teach people how to do Scrum, I often talk about my own personal experience studying the Japanese martial art of aikido over the years.

Scrum, like aikido, or, heck, like the tango, is something that you can only really learn by doing. Your body and your mind and your spirit become aligned through constant practice and improvement. In the martial arts you learn a concept called *Shu Ha Ri*, which points to different levels of mastery. In the *Shu* state you know all the rules and the forms. You repeat them, like the steps in a dance, so your body absorbs them. You don't deviate at all.

In the *Ha* state, once you've mastered the forms, you can make innovations. Put an extra swing in your step down the dance floor.

In the *Ri* state you're able to discard the forms, you've truly mastered the practice, and you're able to be creative in an unhindered way, because the knowledge of the meaning of aikido or the tango is so deeply embedded in you, your every step expresses its essence.

Scrum is a lot like that. It requires practice and attention, but also a continuous effort to reach a new state—a state where things just flow and happen. If you've ever watched great dancers or gymnasts, you know that their motion can almost seem effortless, as if they're doing nothing but simply being. They seem as if they couldn't be anything else but what they are in that moment. I experienced that one day when a diminutive aikido master threw me effortlessly through the air, and yet did so in a way that caused

me to fall gently to the mat, as though I were a baby being gently placed in a cradle.

That's what you want to get to with Scrum. That's the state I want everyone to get to in their lives. Work doesn't have to suck. It can flow; it can be an expression of joy, an alignment toward a higher purpose. We can be better. We can be great! We just have to practice.

For the rest of this book I'm going to spend each chapter focusing on one particular aspect of Scrum. These deep dives are meant to give you the reasoning behind the concepts and why Scrum is structured the way it is. You can find "Implementing Scrum" (a definitive description of Scrum) in the appendix, but it just tells you *what* to do. If you'll come along with me, I'll tell you *why*.

THE TAKEAWAY

Hesitation Is Death. Observe, Orient, Decide, Act. Know where you are, assess your options, make a decision, and act!

Look Outward for Answers. Complex adaptive systems follow a few simple rules, which they learn from their environment.

Great Teams Are. They are cross-functional, autonomous, and empowered, with a transcendent purpose.

Don't Guess. Plan, Do, Check, Act. Plan what you're going to do. Do it. Check whether it did what you wanted. Act on that and change how you're doing things. Repeat in regular cycles, and, by doing so, achieve continuous improvement.

Shu Ha Ri. First, learn the rules and the forms, and once you've mastered them, make innovations. Finally, in a heightened state of mastery, discard the forms and just *be*—with all the learning internalized and decisions made almost unconsciously.

CHAPTER THREE

Teams

Teams are what get things done in the world of work. There are teams that make cars, answer phones, do surgery, program computers, put the news on, and burst through the doors of apartments occupied by terrorists. Certainly, there are artisans or artists who do work by themselves, but teams are what make the world go 'round. And they're what Scrum is based on.

Everyone knows this, but in business we all too often focus solely on individuals, even if production is a team effort. Think of performance bonuses or promotions or hiring. Everything is focused on the individual actor, rather than the team. And that, it turns out, is a big mistake.

Managers tend to focus on the individual because it makes intuitive sense. You want the best people, and people are different, so focus on getting the best performers, and you'll get better results, right? Well, it's not quite that simple.

Take, for example, the process by which students receive grades in a class. At Yale University a computer-programming course taught by Professor Stanley Eisenstat, CS 323, is notoriously hard. When students began complaining about how long each assignment took, the professor didn't make his assignments easier, but he did start tracking how long each student needed to complete them. Then Joel Spolsky, who was in Eisenstat's course back in the 1980s and now has his own software business, compared that data to the actual grades people were getting. He wanted to know if there was any correlation between the time spent on a project and the grade the student received. Interestingly, there *isn't*. Some people work quickly and get an A, and some people work meticulously and get the same grade. The only difference is the amount of time spent. So what is the application for business?

Well, if you're a manager, it seems that you want to hire not just the workers who earn A's, but those who earn them in the shortest amount of time. In the Yale study, the fastest students outpaced their slow compatriots by a ratio of 10:1. They were ten times faster, and they got just as good a grade. Ten times faster is pretty dramatic, right? So it seems that companies should focus on hiring the quickest people and weeding out the slow-footed. That *sounds* like the best approach to increasing productivity, but other factors can be even more crucial.

If you look at teams instead of individuals, you see something interesting. There are studies that looked at some 3,800 different projects, ranging from work done at accounting firms to software development for battleships to tech projects at IBM. The analysts didn't look at individual performance data, but rather team performance data. And when you examine how the teams did, you see something surprising. If the best team could perform a task in one week, how long do you think it took the worst team? You might guess the same ratio as was observed at Yale—10:1 (that is, the slow team took more than two months to accomplish what the fast team knocked off in a week). The actual answer, though, is that there is a much larger difference in team performance than there is in individual performance. It actually didn't take the slow team ten weeks to do what the best team could do in one week. Rather, it took them two *thousand* weeks. That's how great the difference is between the best and the worst. So where should you focus your attention? At the level of the individual, where you might be able to get an improvement of ten times if you can magically make all your employees geniuses? Or at the team level, boosting productivity by an enormous magnitude even if you merely make your worst teams mediocre? Of course, aiming for mediocrity will get you just that. But what if you could make all your teams great?

At certain times in certain places with certain small groups of people, everything becomes possible. Even if you've never been on a team like that, you've seen them in action. You hear stories about them; legends are told about what they can do. I grew up near Boston and live there now, so some of the great teams that come to my mind are the Celtics of the 1980s or the New England Patriots of the Tom Brady era. When those teams were on, it seemed as if they were playing a different game than everyone else. Drives and plays that had once seemed undoable suddenly became part of the game plan. It was as if a state of grace had descended upon those players, and for a moment they could do no wrong. Larry Bird would drive down the court and pass the ball without looking toward what seemed to be empty hardwood. But just as the ball was headed out of bounds, Kevin McHale would simply *appear* exactly where he was supposed to be. And then he'd throw the ball to the side—again, seemingly without looking—and Robert Parish would just happen to be perfectly positioned for a shot. That absolute alignment of purpose and trust is something that creates greatness.

We've all seen those teams. Some of us have been lucky to be on one—or *more* than one—over the course of our lives. When I was designing Scrum, I looked at what super-performing teams had that other teams didn't. Why is it, I wondered, that some teams change the world, and others are mired in mediocrity? What are the common elements that truly great teams have? And, most important, can we reproduce them?

The answer, it turns out, is yes.

In their original paper that described what became Scrum, "The New New Product Development Game," Professors Takeuchi and Nonaka described the characteristics of the teams they saw at the best companies in the world:

1. **Transcendent:** They have a sense of purpose beyond the ordinary. This self-realized goal allows them to move beyond the ordinary into the extraordinary. In a very real way the very decision to not be average, but to be great, changes the way they view themselves, and what they're capable of.

2. **Autonomous:** The teams are self-organizing and self-managing, they have the power to make their own decisions about how they do their jobs, and are empowered to make those decisions stick.

3. **Cross-Functional:** The teams have all the skills needed to complete the project. Planning, design, production, sales, distribution. And those skills feed and reinforce each other. As one team member that designed a revolutionary new camera for Canon described it: "When all the team members are located in one large room, someone's information becomes yours, without even trying. You then start thinking in terms of what's best or second best for the group at large and not only where you stand."[1]

So how do you create a team that aims for a higher goal, organizes itself, and constantly feeds off each member's skills? I spent a lot of time pondering that. After all, you can't just yell at people to be more self-organized and transcendent; the motivation has to come from within. Imposing it will kill what you're trying to do. Might there be a simple set of rules that encourage the formation of magic?

The Long Gray Line

I thought back to when I was part of one of those magical teams. It was in the early 1960s, when I was a cadet at the United States Military Academy, more commonly known as West Point. During my last year there I was appointed as training officer to my cadet company, L2, the "Loose Deuce."

In 1963, there were twenty-four companies at West Point. A1 through M1 and A2 through M2. Three times a week these companies took to the parade field and marched in full dress uniform, with rifles held thus and swords so, and white straps here, and gear placed carefully there. These parade formations have been a competition at the Academy for almost two hundred years. In 1963, the Loose Deuce had been at the bottom of those rankings for more than a century.

The training officer has no direct power. He isn't part of the command structure of the company. No one answers to him. No one has to do what he says. But after each parade the training officers get together and rate each company according to various criteria. As training officer of the Loose Deuce, I decided that what I could do was make things more transparent. I made colored charts of what went right and what went wrong and posted them in the barracks where everyone in my company would have to see them every day.

At first the criticisms were simple. *Charlie had his sword stuck in the dirt. Jim didn't turn in sync with everyone else. Dave's salute was sloppy.* There were no punishments or blame; it was simply facts laid out by all the other training officers that were brought up during evaluations. Yet these were the reasons L2 was rated at the bottom.

Within just a few weeks the cadets sharpened their game, and the low ratings now pointed to the company commander. His orders weren't clear enough; the timing wasn't crisp enough. Not surprisingly, I got heat for criticizing the commander, but I said simply in response, "The ratings are the ratings. I'm just showing you what they are. The ranks have pulled their shit together. *You* are now the problem. Do you want to fix it? Or do you want to suck forever?" A few weeks later L2 was the number one company at West Point.

The most honored cadet in West Point's history was General Douglas MacArthur. He had the highest ranking of any cadet who graduated there, and he was a leading officer in both World Wars. As a five-star general and Medal of Honor winner, he had a special connection to the Corps of Cadets.

The year before I was training my company, in May of 1962, he gave his final speech at West Point. You have to picture the scene properly to get the full impact. There were three thousand men in cadet gray uniforms sitting in this gargantuan stone hall with vast columns and giant chandeliers hanging from the high ceiling. About thirty feet up on one wall was a platform that overlooked the hall. General MacArthur, then frail, stood on that platform and gave what today is referred to as the "Long Gray Line" speech (gray being the color of the cadets' uniforms):

You are the leaven which binds together the entire fabric of our national system of defense. From your ranks come the great captains who hold the Nation's destiny in their hands the moment the war tocsin sounds.

The long gray line has never failed us. Were you to do so, a million ghosts in olive drab, in brown khaki, in blue and gray, would rise from their white crosses, thundering those magic words: Duty, Honor, Country.[2]

At that, I remember, it felt as if a legion of those ghosts rose up behind MacArthur as he left the Corps with his final charge. And three thousand men, trained for war, to whom tears did not come easily, began to cry.

In my dreams I hear again the crash of guns, the rattle of musketry, the strange, mournful mutter of the battlefield. But in the evening of my memory I come back to West Point. Always there echoes and re-echoes: Duty, Honor, Country.

Today marks my final roll call with you. But I want you to know that when I cross the river, my last conscious thoughts will be of the Corps, and the Corps, and the Corps.[3]

To this day, every cadet at the Academy has to memorize that speech, line by line, word for word, before they can graduate. That speech has become the spiritual guide for the cadet corps, and for the US officer corps at large: Duty, Honor, Country.

Almost a year after that speech General MacArthur died. One company was selected to march at his funeral. To the slow, rhythmic sound of the drums, the Loose Deuce, the same company that had been the worst in the Corps for more than a hundred years, marched behind the caisson carrying the casket of one of America's greatest generals.

A few months after that funeral I marched with the Loose Deuce for the last time at my graduation. All twenty-four companies marched, but L2, because of our position in the alphabet, marched twenty-third. After the ceremony my future father-in-law asked me, "That company. The second to last one. They were different than all the rest. The others were marching; they seemed to be floating. Who were they?"

"That was my company," I told him. "Those men buried General MacArthur."

My company had achieved transcendence.

Scrum in the Time of Revolt

Often when people talk about great teams, they *only* talk about that transcendent sense of purpose. But while that's a critical element, it's only one leg of the three-legged stool. Just as critical, but perhaps less celebrated, is the freedom to do your job in the way that you think best—to have autonomy. On all great teams, it's left to the members to decide how to carry out the goals set by those leading the organization.

Tahrir Square has become synonymous with the Egyptian revolution and the ongoing struggles in that country, but before January of 2011 it was just another dirty, traffic-clogged rotary in downtown Cairo. To the north lies the rose-red Egyptian Museum and to the south the high walls of the American University in Cairo and the iconic Muqawama government building. The headquarters of the National Democratic Party of the Egyptian dictator Hosni Mubarak was on the west, as was the Arab League headquarters.

Oddly, at the square's eastern edge was, of all things, a KFC, which soon became the backdrop to stone-throwing protestors pushing back police.

In late January of 2011 a small group of protesters decided to demonstrate within the traffic circle to protest the brutal killing of a young man named Khaled Said by Egyptian police. What might have been another small protest against a repressive regime caught fire, ignited the Egyptian imagination, and eventually drew millions to the square. Over the next month the unthinkable happened. Just by people gathering and saying no, one of the oldest and most powerful dictatorial regimes in the Middle East fell. The people gathered day after day, night after night, filling the square and creating an alternate country where the dictator Hosni Mubarak did not rule and individuals could actually speak their minds. They changed their world.

For journalists it was a massive story of historical significance. Among those descending on Cairo was National Public Radio, one of the premier journalism outfits in the United States. Caught flat-footed at first, producers and reporters for NPR blew deadlines, missed stories, and scrambled to meet the demands of executives back in Washington.

J. J. Sutherland, my son, was sent to fix it. A longtime war producer and correspondent, he was assigned to Cairo to make the coverage work. The story was too big not to be on the air every single day, every single show, and every single hour. J.J. dropped down into a country where the airports had been closed, foreigners were desperately trying to flee, and the cell phone network and Internet had been shut down. He was the senior producer on the scene, but, much like a training officer at West Point, an NPR producer is a facilitator and organizer—a helper or booster rather than a typical manager or leader. J.J.'s job was to help the team do the best work they could. It wasn't to *tell* them what to do—rather, it was to provide them with what they needed. The orders from management were to tell the story and to be on the air multiple times a day, and the team on the ground figured out how to meet that challenge, deciding what stories to tell and how to tell them using the medium of radio.

Oddly, it was precisely because it was so difficult to communicate with executives back in Washington that the team was so successful. In a very real way, they were on their own. With constant direct oversight by Washington being impossible and events happening so fast, the team had to organize themselves to get the work done. One of the key concepts in Scrum is that the team members decide *themselves* how they're going to do the work. It's management's responsibility to set the strategic goals, but it's the team's job to decide how to reach those goals. In Cairo, there was no way anyone *not* on the ground could even keep up with what was happening. Almost daily the NPR team would report a series of stories for the next day that would be rendered instantly obsolete by rapidly unfolding events. There'd be a major clash in the square, a speech, a resignation, or a battle, and all the team's work would be for naught. Suddenly, they'd be scrambling to get something timely on the air.

They succeeded by using Scrum. Their deadlines called for them to report every twelve hours, on *Morning Edition* and *All Things Considered*. Each cycle J.J. would talk to the team and ask three very simple questions: What did you do since the last time we talked? What are you going to do before we talk again? And what is getting in your way? His asking those questions, which is one of the regular rituals of Scrum, forced the correspondents to talk and share with one another. And J.J.'s main job, as de facto Scrum Master, was to make sure that those things getting in the team's way at one meeting were gone by the next. The impediment could be anything—from dealing with Egyptian bureaucracy to getting a secure hotel room, from finding drivers and translators to getting correspondents out of the custody of Egypt's feared secret police, the Mukhabarat.

How did it all work out? Well, what had begun in chaos, personal disputes, and a failure to deliver the news quickly became a well-oiled machine that management didn't even have to manage. Instead, team members managed themselves. Over the next few weeks NPR's squad in Cairo produced more coverage than anyone thought possible. And it was of higher quality than what the competition was offering, eventually winning several awards. It was a feat that wouldn't have been accomplished had the team not been imbued with a sense of purpose (to tell one of the biggest stories of their careers) and not possessed autonomy (the ability to decide for themselves how to produce the many threads of that overall story).

Now Scrum is being used all over the place at NPR, from web design, to data journalism, to creating new radio shows. Teams at the *Chicago Tribune, New York Times, Washington Post,* and *ProPublica* are all using Scrum. When deadlines are tight, they just need the speed.

One Team to Get the Job Done

The third leg of the stool for great teams is that they have all the skills necessary to get things done. In a classically organized structure you might have the team of planners, followed by the team of builders, followed by the team of testers, followed by the production team, followed by the shipping team. Each team along the way has to finish its piece of the action before the project can move to the next step. No one team by itself can actually get a product out the door.

The classic example of this was NASA's "phase-gate" process. This was how they ran the shuttle program and other efforts in the sixties, seventies, and eighties. It's very different now, but here's how their old process worked. First, there's a discovery "phase," where people decide what they're going to try to accomplish— maybe it's build a rocket that goes to the moon. A bunch of strategists sit in a room and fantasize about it. Then there's a "gate," where a manager or group of managers has to sign off on the project as worthy of pursuing. Then there's a scoping phase, where all the "requirements people" decide what the thing is going to do. Then there's another gate, and another set of meetings, and then these humongous documents are handed off to the next phase, building the business case and the project plan. Then all these plans are taken to another set of meetings and approvals and, after that, handed off to yet *another* phase, the development phase, where the thing is actually built. Then there's another bunch of meetings and documents, and the product is handed off to a whole other group for the next phase, testing. Those people have never seen the product before, but they test it, sign off that it's right, and then push it to another gate, or set of interminable meetings, with another bunch of documents that no one has read. And then and only then is the product passed to a *sixth* group of people who'll actually launch it. It's exhausting just writing about it. And this is how NASA used to build things.

At one point in the early 1980s, executives from Fuji-Xerox traveled to America to study how the famous space agency did things. When they implemented the same procedures back in Japan, they immediately saw quality drop, the failure rate go up, and their ability to deliver sink like a stone. They quickly abandoned the process, saying it was likely to produce catastrophic error. The Rogers Commission that examined the 1986 *Challenger* disaster agreed. As physicist Richard Feynman famously wrote in Appendix F of the Commission's report: "It would appear that, for whatever purpose, be it for internal or external consumption, the management of NASA exaggerates the reliability of its product, to the point of fantasy."[4]

The fact is, when you look at the best teams—like the ones that existed at Toyota or 3M when Takeuchi or Nonaka wrote their paper, or the ones at Google or Salesforce.com or Amazon today—there isn't this separation of roles. Each team has all the people on it do everything, soup to nuts.

Nicola Dourambeis is in charge of Agile practices at Salesforce.com. She's responsible for some two hundred Scrum teams at a company that is routinely on such lists as *Fortune*'s "100 Best Companies to Work For" and *Forbes*'s "Most Innovative Companies in the World." She says she sees Scrum as their "secret sauce." "When we were a start-up," she says, "we did a major release three or four times a year. As we grew and scaled up, managing projects in a typical waterfall way, that fell to once a year in 2005–2006. That had to change. So we introduced Scrum. Since then we've been doing releases three times a year. There aren't that many major enterprise companies that can do that."

What she looks for in a team is diversity—of skill set, thinking, and experience. She wants teams that are unselfish and autonomous, but she also needs them to be cross-functional. Teams that can get a whole project done.

One of her tests of whether a team is on the right path comes when she asks, say, a network engineer, "What team are you on?"

If he or she responds by mentioning the product they're working on (say automation or integration) rather than their specialty (such as network engineering), she nods approvingly. When a specialist identifies with their specialty more than with the product they're actually making, Dourambeis knows she still has work to do.

Scrum at War

One of the most dramatic examples of a cross-functional team comes from the military. American Special Operations Forces (SOF) operate in just this way. A typical Army Special Forces "A-team" has twelve people: a team leader (who is a commissioned officer), a warrant officer, a team sergeant (who runs the team in day-to-day operations), an intelligence sergeant, and two each of sergeants in special forces weapons, demolition, medical, and communications. Each team has all the capabilities to carry out their mission from start to finish. And they conduct cross-training across each skill set. They want to make sure, for example, that if both of the medics get killed, the communications specialist can patch up the weapons specialist. Another way the Special Forces operate is that, unlike much of the "regular" military, they don't separate intelligence gathering and operations planning. There are no hand-offs from one team to another, where mistakes might be made. Special Forces don't want any *Challenger* disasters. As a result there's constant communication among the people collecting the intelligence, those planning what to do with it, and those who'll be going through the door.

During the Iraq war, Special Forces teams showed that they were exceedingly good at killing people. They could locate an insurgent target and wipe it out that same night. Between 2003 and

2007 they carried out thousands of successful missions aimed at disrupting the Iraqi insurgency, especially Al Qaeda in Iraq. Tactically and operationally, they almost always succeeded in their missions. Their cross-functional, highly trained teams were among the most lethal forces the world had ever seen. Yet despite all their skill and talent they had almost zero strategic impact. During those first four years of the war, attacks on American forces and Iraqi civilians increased almost daily. During some of the darkest days of the war there were over one hundred attacks a day on American forces, and even the lethality of the American Special Forces couldn't stem the tide. By late 2006 and early 2007 just about every informed commentator saw Iraq as a lost cause. Every additional American death started to be seen as a futile sacrifice.

Then in 2007 General David Petraeus led what became known as the "Surge," which involved putting tens of thousands more troops into the country and having them live among the populace. This new strategy had a remarkable impact. One reason was that it got the Iraqi people to believe that the Americans were on their side, fighting the insurgents who were blowing up bombs in their neighborhoods and conducting ethnic cleansing. Another reason was that the American military, using a program called the "Sons of Iraq," succeeded in bribing tens of thousands of former insurgents to come over to the US side. But there was a third component of the strategy—something that journalist Bob Woodward called as revolutionary as the invention of the tank or the airplane.

This weapon wasn't a new gizmo or unmanned drone. It was what General Stanley McChrystal, the commander of the Joint Special Operations Command at the time, called "collaborative warfare." It involved using cross-functional teams from across the entire US government to target and disrupt Al Qaeda networks. As the *Washington Post* described it on September 6, 2008:

The CIA [Central Intelligence Agency] provides intelligence analysts and spy craft with sensors and cameras that can track targets, vehicles or equipment for up to 14 hours. FBI [Federal Bureau of Investigation] forensic experts dissect data, from cell-phone information to the "pocket litter" found on extremists. Treasury officials track funds flowing among extremists and from governments. National Security Agency staffers intercept conversations and computer data, and members of the National Geospatial-Intelligence Agency use high-tech equipment to pinpoint where suspected extremists are using phones or computers.[5]

What they did was create a cross-functional team that had all the skills necessary to get the job done. Instead of having all these experts on separate teams rarely sharing information, they all worked together, in the same room, sharing all their intelligence and planning to track down and kill Al Qaeda operatives.

Before this, an intelligence organization would designate the target, then hand off the actual operations to a Special Forces team. Then that team would hand over any intelligence it gathered to yet another team for analysis. Those practicing the handoff model discovered what Fuji-Xerox discovered decades earlier when the Japanese tried to implement NASA's phase-gate system, and it's one of the main reasons Scrum was developed in the first place. Whenever there are handoffs between teams, there is the opportunity for disaster. As an article titled "Employing ISR: SOF Best Practices" in *Joint Force Quarterly* put it:

The interagency teams made it possible to eliminate the organizational seams between the different coalition actors in Iraq, placing an "unblinking eye" on high-value targets. . . . Passing responsibilities between units and organizations represented an "organizational blink" during which momentum slowed and the target might escape.[6]

Sharing information and resources like this isn't easy in any setting. I've seen managers almost seize up as their resources are assigned to a team outside their direct control. Giving up day-to-day micromanaging and control is hard to do, but to do it in the secretive world of intelligence and special operations is even more difficult—so difficult that, despite their effectiveness, the teams in Iraq were quickly disbanded after the Surge was deemed a success. Christopher Lamb and Evan Munsing wrote a fascinating article, "Secret Weapon: High-value Target Teams as an Organizational Innovation," laying this out.

> . . . as soon as the near-failure in Iraq was averted, bureaucratic support for interagency teams began to decline. By 2008, other departments and agencies, particularly one unidentified intelligence agency, began pulling back people and cooperation, believing information-sharing and collaboration had gone too far.[7]

The most powerful weapon in America's arsenal, what Bob Woodward called as important as the invention of the tank or the airplane, was set aside because of parochial departmental concerns and the worries of middle managers who were concerned for their careers. I've seen this happen at one large financial institution in Boston repeatedly. They'll call me up in a panic when they have a mission-critical project that is in trouble. They'll have me train dozens of their people in Scrum, have me start up teams that are capable of addressing their emergency. They direct people from across the organization into cross-functional teams to address the issue. And then they solve it. Once the crisis is past, they disband the teams to their respective silos and managerial fiefdoms. The transparency and sharing of a truly fantastic team threatens structures rooted in secrets and obfuscation. Managers often don't want other managers, their own teams, or other people within the power structure to know exactly what they're doing or what is being accomplished and how fast. They see keeping that knowledge secret as critical to their power. Instead of being aligned with the interests of the greater good, they're aligned with their own motivations, which often boil down to greed and ambition. It's the same kind of thinking that led to the massive management failure that caused the most recent economic collapse. At many companies, actions were based solely on what was in it for the individual on a short-term basis. There was no thought of what would benefit everyone, or of limiting harm to the global economy.

Size Does Matter, but Not the Way You Think

But just because cross-functionality can achieve great results, you shouldn't play Noah and throw two of everything into a team. The team dynamic only works well in *small* teams. The classic formulation is seven people, plus or minus two, though I've seen teams as small as three function at a high level. What's fascinating is that the data shows that if you have more than nine people on a team, their velocity actually slows down. That's right. More resources make the team go slower.

In software development there's a term called "Brooks's Law" that Fred Brooks first coined back in 1975 in his seminal book *The Mythical Man-Month*. Put simply, Brooks's Law says "adding manpower to a late software project makes it later."[8] This has been borne out in study after study. Lawrence Putnam is a legendary figure in software development, and he has made it his life's work to study how long things take to make and why. His work kept showing that projects with twenty or more people on them used more effort than those with five or fewer. Not just a little bit, but a lot. A large team would take about five times the number of hours that a small team would. He saw this again and again, and in the mid-1990s he decided to try to do a broad-based study to determine what the right team size is. So he looked at 491 medium-size projects at hundreds of different companies. These were all projects that required new products or features to be created, not a repurposing of old versions. He divided the projects by team size and noticed something right away. Once the teams grew larger than eight, they took dramatically longer to get things done. Groups made up of three to seven people required about 25 percent of the effort of groups of nine to twenty to get the same amount of work done. This result recurred over hundreds and hundreds of projects. That very large groups do *less* seems to be an ironclad rule of human nature.

But why? To answer that, we have to look at the limitations of the human brain. You've probably heard of the classic George Miller study in 1956 showing that the maximum number of items the average person can retain in their short-term memory is seven. This is supposedly why telephone numbers are seven numbers long. The problem with Miller's work is that later research has proved him wrong.

In 2001, Nelson Cowan of the University of Missouri wondered whether that magic rule of seven was really true and conducted a wide survey of all the new research on the topic. It turns out that the number of items one can retain in short-term memory isn't seven. It's four.[9] People often think that they can memorize more than that, using a mnemonic device or by just concentrating harder. But the research is fairly clear that we can only remember four "chunks" of data. The classic example is giving someone the following series of twelve letters: *fbicbsibmirs*. People can usually remember about four of those letters—*unless* they notice that they can be "chunked" into well-known acronyms: FBI, CBS, IBM, IRS. If you can link things in your short-term memory to long-term memory associations, you can hold more. But the part of the mind that focuses—the conscious part—can only hold about four distinct items at once.

So there's a hardwired limit to what our brain can hold at any one time. Which leads us back to Brooks. When he tried to figure out why adding more people to a project made it take longer, he discovered two reasons. The first is the time it takes to bring people up to speed. As you'd expect, bringing a new person up to speed slows down everyone else. The second reason has to do not only with *how* we think but, quite literally, with *what* our brains are capable of thinking. The number of communication channels increases dramatically with the number of people, and our brains just can't handle it.

If you want to calculate the impact of group size, you take the number of people on a team, multiply by "that number minus one," and divide by two. Communication channels = $n(n-1)/2$. So, for example, if you have five people, you have ten channels. Six people, fifteen channels. Seven, twenty-one. Eight, twenty-eight. Nine, thirty-six. Ten, forty-five. Our brains simply can't keep up with that many people at once. We don't know what everyone is doing. And we slow down as we try to figure it out.

Just as on a Special Forces team, everyone on a Scrum team has to know what everyone else is doing. All the work being done, the challenges faced, the progress made, has to be transparent to everyone else. And if the team gets too big, the ability of everyone to communicate clearly with everyone else, all the time, gets muddled. There are too many crosscurrents. Often, the team socially and functionally breaks into sub-teams that begin working at cross-purposes. The cross-functionality is lost. Meetings that took minutes now take hours.

Don't do it. Keep your teams small.

The Scrum Master

With the first Scrum team, I regularly showed them a video of the All Blacks rugby team getting ready for a game. The All Blacks, a legendary team from the small country of New Zealand, are a transcendent team. Before every game they perform the Maori warrior ceremony of the *haka*. The *haka* is a warrior dance that charges up people about to go into battle. While watching it, you can almost see the energy come out of each player and coalesce into a greater whole. With synchronized stomping and clapping and chanting—ritualized movements of cutting an enemy's throat—you can see ordinary men transform themselves into something bigger, something greater. They're invoking a warrior spirit that does not accept defeat or dismay.

It took a few viewings of the video, but my team of slightly-out-of-shape computer programmers eventually started to talk about how *they* could be that way. They came up with four aspects worthy of emulation. The first was intense focus on the goal, built up and energized by the Maori chant. The second was radical collaboration—arms and bodies locked together, pushing for the same goal. The third was hunger to crush—anything in their way was to be obliterated. The fourth was universal excitement when any team member broke through with the ball. Who it was didn't matter. That it happened was cause for celebration.

So we set up this framework of Sprints and Daily Stand-up meetings and Reviews and Retrospectives, and I realized we needed someone whose job it was to make sure the process itself was effective. Not a manager—more of a servant-leader, something between a team captain and a coach. As we were watching the All Blacks every day, I asked the team what we should call this person. They decided on "Scrum Master." He or she would facilitate all the meetings, make sure there was transparency, and, most important, help the team discover what was getting in their way. The key part of that was to realize that often the impediments aren't simply that the machine doesn't work or that Jim in accounting is a jerk—it's the process itself. It was the Scrum Master's job to guide the team toward *continuous improvement*—to ask with regularity, "How can we do what we do better?"

Ideally, at the end of each iteration, each Sprint, the team would look closely at itself—at its interactions, practices, and processes—and ask two questions: "What can we change about how we work?" and "What is our biggest sticking point?" If those questions are answered forthrightly, a team can go faster than anyone ever imagined.

Don't Hate the Player, Hate the Game

It often turns out that low team morale, cohesion, and productivity are based on a fundamental misunderstanding of how humans work. How many times have you gotten together with a colleague and started bitching about a third who "isn't pulling her weight" or "always slows us down" or "makes stupid decisions"? Or have you been with a group confronting a problem and the first thing that everyone does is try to fix blame?

I'm willing to bet each and every one of you has been in a meeting like that. I'd also bet that each and every one of you, at one time or another, has been the person who has ended up being blamed for the problem. But I'd also be willing to bet that when you're blaming someone, you're finding fault with them personally, while if *you* are being blamed, you're much more aware of the situational factors that led to the problem and why you acted the way you did. And you know what? When you're talking about yourself, you're absolutely right. When talking about others, though, you're making one of the most common—and destructive—human errors in judging other people's actions. It even has a name: "Fundamental Attribution Error."

Some fascinating studies related to this are laid out in the book *Induction: Processes of Inference, Learning, and Discovery,* by John H. Holland et al. One paper cited in the book was published in the early 1970s, so this isn't new. This is old stuff that has been reproduced over and over and over again. It's all about what makes humans tick. Anyway, this group of researchers gathered together a bunch of male college students and asked them a couple of simple questions: "Why did you choose your major?" and "Why are you dating the person you are?" And then the researchers asked their subjects to answer the same questions about their best friend. Important differences emerged. When the students talked about themselves, they talked not about themselves personally but, rather, what they were asked about. They said such things as, "Chemistry is a high-paying field" about their major, and "She's a very warm person" about their girlfriend. But when they talked about their friends, they talked about their friends' abilities and needs—things such as, "He was always good at math," or "He's kind of dependent and needs a take-charge kind of woman."[10]

This way of perceiving the world is funny when you see it in others. It's so obvious that they're making misjudgments. But before you laugh, you need to own up that *you* do it all the time as well. Everyone does. We all perceive ourselves as responding to a situation, while we see others as motivated by their character. One amusing side effect is that when we're asked to report on our personality traits and those of our friends, we always paint ourselves as far more boring. We say we have dramatically fewer character traits than our friends.

The authors of *Induction* draw an interesting parallel between how we think mistakenly about social motivations and how nonscientists or people with merely an intuitive understanding of physics view the physical world.

An intuitive physicist might explain why a rock falls by saying the rock itself has the intrinsic quality of gravity, rather than saying that gravity is part of a system of forces acting on the rock. In the same way, when we talk about others, we talk about their inherent properties, rather than see those properties in relation to the external environment. In fact, it's those interactions with our environment that drive our behavior. It's *the system that surrounds us,* rather than any intrinsic quality, that accounts for the vast majority of our behavior. What Scrum is designed to do is change that system. Instead of looking for blame and fault, it rewards positive behavior by focusing people on working together and getting things done.

Perhaps the most famous demonstration of this human reaction to systems was the Milgram experiment on obedience to authority figures, which was done in the early 1960s at Yale University. The experiment was simple and, to modern eyes, somewhat cruel. It was also devastating and powerful and is taught in every first-year psychology course. Dr. Stanley Milgram, a professor at Yale, had a question that was quite apropos then. Three months before the first experiments began, Adolf Eichmann, the architect of the Holocaust, went on trial.

One of the most persistent questions surrounding the Holocaust was how so many millions of people could have been willing accomplices in such horror. Were Germans fundamentally morally reprehensible? Was there something intrinsically evil within their cultural makeup? Or were they really just following orders? It's very easy to look at crimes against humanity and blame individuals for their actions. It's the right thing to do, no? The question that Milgram wanted to answer, though, is: Are ordinary Americans so different from Germans? Would they have reacted differently in the same situation? And the uncomfortable answer is that no, Americans *wouldn't* have behaved differently. In fact, given how many countries and cultures have replicated the experiment, *no one* would have. Given the right situation, we're all capable of being Nazis.

The experiment worked this way. The subject, an ordinary person, was told by someone wearing a white lab coat (which gave him a veneer of scientific authority) to administer ever-greater electrical shocks to a third person, an actor, who was in another room. The subject could hear but not see the actor. As the shocks increased, the actor would begin to scream and shout and beg. Eventually the actor (who in some versions of the experiment told the subject he had a heart condition) would start banging on the wall, yelling for the experiment to stop. Finally, he would go silent.

Some people paused at 135 volts, as the actor screamed, and asked about the purpose of the experiment. Almost all continued after they were assured that they wouldn't be held responsible. Some subjects began to laugh nervously as they heard the cries of agony from the next room. When the subject wanted to stop, the "scientist" simply said, "Please *continue*." And if the subject wouldn't, the scientist would go on, "The experiment requires that you *continue*." If still nothing, the scientist would add, "It is absolutely essential that you *continue*." Most subjects appeared to be under great stress and sweated profusely. They exhibited an elevated pulse and temperature as the "fight-or-flight" instinct took hold. And then, if they still wouldn't press the button, the scientist would try one last time. "You have no other choice. You *must* go on."

Almost everyone did, delivering the final shock to someone who'd been screaming and then gone silent. Milgram summarized the implications this way in his 1974 article "The Perils of Obedience":

> Ordinary people, simply doing their jobs, and without any particular hostility on their part, can become agents in a terrible destructive process. Moreover, even when the destructive effects of their work become patently clear, and they are asked to carry out actions incompatible with fundamental standards of morality, relatively few people have the resources needed to resist authority.[11]

When this experiment is discussed in classrooms, it is usually pointed out to students that it is the *system* within which those ordinary people were operating that was the culprit, rather than the people themselves. But it's a hard lesson to internalize, because if you accept the truth of that, what does it say about you?

What it says is that we're *all* creatures of the system we find ourselves embedded in. What Scrum does is accept this reality, and, instead of seeking someone to blame, it tries to examine the system that produced the failure and fix it.

Another experiment that illuminates a similar phenomenon was carried out at a theological seminary in the early seventies. You'd think that seminarians would be the most compassionate people on the planet, right? The subjects of the experiment were told that they had to give a sermon on the other side of campus. Some were told they had to hurry, because people were already waiting for them, and they were late. Others weren't told to hurry. As they made their way across the school grounds, each seminarian passed someone moaning for help in a doorway. How many of the people who were told they had to hurry stopped to help? Ten percent. Of *seminarians*.

Yet people want to blame individuals, not systems. It just feels better. The Fundamental Attribution Error appeals to our sense of justice. If we can blame someone else, we insulate ourselves from the possibility that we'd do the same thing—that we're just as likely to press that button as anyone else, given the right circumstances.

How does this error of blaming individuals rather than systems manifest in business? I have two good examples, the first being the New United Motor Manufacturing, Inc., (NUMMI) automotive plant in Fremont, California. It was a joint venture between General Motors and Toyota. The plant was closed by GM in 1982.

Management considered the workforce the worst in America. People drank on the job, didn't show up for work, and subtly sabotaged the cars (by, for example, putting a Coke bottle inside a door, where it would rattle and annoy customers). Toyota reopened the plant in 1984. GM told them about how awful the workers were but that the managers were great and they should rehire them. Instead, Toyota declined to rehire the managers and rehired most of the original workforce—even sent some of them to Japan to learn the Toyota Production System. Almost immediately the NUMMI plant was producing cars with the same precision and as few defects as cars that were produced in Japan. Same people, different system. GM never reached those levels of quality at any of its other American plants. It pulled out of the joint operating agreement the same year it went bankrupt.

The second example that comes to mind is slightly different. It reminds me of how much of a "default position" it is for people to start looking for someone to blame for a problem rather than search for a solution. It has to do with how the venture capitalists I work with operate when they decide to invest in a company. I was surprised when I first joined OpenView Venture Partners that, unlike many VC firms, they don't really care how the company spent the money they had *before* their investment. History doesn't matter. OpenView decides whether to spend money based on a firm's current state—everything else is immaterial. They want to know how *their* money is going to be spent. How the company spent the other guys' money isn't important. It's only the future—only the *solutions*—that matter.

Reaching "Great"

When a team starts to align and synchronize, it can seem magical. You feel it when you walk into a room with them. You see it as they take the field. They look as if they're floating; they've become greater than themselves.

I was at a friend's house recently in Copenhagen. As you can imagine, since he's European, he's a major soccer fan. I'm not sure what tournament his favorite team was playing in, but it was intense, watching him jump up and down and scream at the television. This was a sports fan in high dudgeon. And then came this moment: the score was tied, the seconds were ticking down, and his team had the ball. From maybe a quarter of the way down the field, *without looking at where his teammates were,* a forward kicked the ball into a mass of players in front of the goal. The problem was, none were on the kicker's team. For an instant I felt deflated; then, suddenly, a player on my friend's team appeared—at just the right place and time, and headed the ball into the goal. The player had run full speed from midfield into the mass of opponents in front of the goal, where he seized the opportunity to head the ball. It was a total surprise. The forward who'd originally kicked the ball had faith, though, that his teammate would be where he was supposed to be. And that teammate had faith that the ball would be placed where he could do something with it. It was the kind of synchronicity that is inspiring to watch.

And that's a place I want to help people reach with Scrum. It's not impossible. It's not only the elites and athletes and special people who can do this. It's about setting up the right framework with the right incentives and giving people the freedom, respect, and authority to do things themselves. Greatness can't be imposed; it has to come from within. But it does live within all of us.

SCRUM

THE TAKEAWAY

Pull the Right Lever. Change Team performance. That has *much* more impact—by several orders of magnitude—than individual performance.

Transcendence. Great teams have a purpose that is greater than the individual; e.g., burying General MacArthur, winning the NBA championship.

Autonomy. Give teams the freedom to make decisions on how to take action—to be respected as masters of their craft. The ability to improvise will make all the difference, whether the unit is reporting on a revolution in the Middle East or making a sale.

Cross-functional. The team must have every skill needed to complete a project, whether the mission is to deliver Salesforce.com software or capture terrorists in Iraq.

Small Wins. Small teams get work done faster than big teams. The rule of thumb is seven team members—plus or minus two. Err on the small side.

Blame Is Stupid. Don't look for bad people; look for bad systems—ones that incentivize bad behavior and reward poor performance.

CHAPTER FOUR

Time

Time is the ultimate limiter of human endeavor, affecting everything from how much we work, to how long things take, to how successful we are. The relentless one-way flow of time fundamentally shapes how we view the world and ourselves. As the seventeenth-century British poet Andrew Marvell famously put it, "Had we but world enough, and time" anything could be accomplished. But, of course, a sense of mortality hovers over our every effort. We know our time is limited. As such, isn't it the greatest of crimes to waste it? Marvell, again:

> *Thus, though we cannot make our sun*
> *Stand still, yet we will make him run.*[1]

But how do we do that? It's easy enough to shout "Carpe diem!" from a stage to inspire a crowd, but how do you actually pull it off? A lot of work is telling people to sit down, buckle up, and put in long hours. "Don't think about the outside world," our bosses tell us implicitly. "Don't worry about your kids, going surfing, or even dinner—just work, and then work harder, and you'll be rewarded. You'll get that promotion. You'll make that sale. You'll finish that project."

While I have nothing against promotions, sales, or projects, it's just a fact that humans are absolutely terrible at working that way. We're lousy focusers, we spend far more hours in the office than needed, and we're horrible estimators of how long things will take. This is *all* people I'm talking about—it's how we humans simply *are*.

When I sat down to develop Scrum, I had no intention of creating a new "process." I simply wanted to gather together all the research that had been done for decades on how people work best and emulate that. I wanted to incorporate best practices and steal any better ideas I came across. Right before the first real Scrum at Easel in 1993 I was working at a company just blocks from the MIT Media Lab, and I stole an idea from the lab that has become the core of Scrum: the Sprint.

The Sprint

In the early 1990s the Media Lab was coming up with all sorts of neat stuff. This was during the time that the World Wide Web was being birthed, and they were doing everything from robots to the electronic ink that makes e-readers possible to new ways to encode sound. It was an incredibly heady time, and I tended to hire students coming out of the lab because they were chock-full of ideas, had an incredible ability to make things that were cool, and they could build them fast.

Their speed owed itself to a policy that the Media Lab had for all its projects. Every three weeks each team had to demonstrate to their colleagues what it was working on. This was an open demonstration; anyone could come. And if that demo wasn't both working and cool, lab directors killed the project. This forced the students to build neat stuff fast and, most important, to get immediate feedback on it.

Think about many of the projects that you do. I'd bet that you seldom get feedback on them until completion—and that could be months, even years, away. You might be heading *completely* in the wrong direction for months and not suspect it. That's throwing huge chunks of your life away. In business it could mean the difference between success and failure. I see this happen all the time: a company will spend years on a project that seemed like a good idea when the workers started on it, but by the time they cross the finish line, the market has fundamentally changed. The sooner you give things to your customers, the quicker they can tell you if you're making something they need.

So when I started the first Scrum at Easel and told the CEO I wasn't going to show him a long and detailed Gantt chart that we both knew was wrong, he said, "Fine. What *are* you going to show me?" And I told him that each month I'd show him a piece of working software. Not something that works in the back end. Not some piece of architecture. A piece of software that a customer can actually use. A fully implemented feature.

"Okay," he said. "Do that."

And so my team embarked on what we called "Sprints." We called them that because the name evoked a quality of intensity. We were going to work all out for a short period of time and then stop to see where we were.

"Team WIKISPEED" is a group founded by the wonderfully named Joe Justice. They make cars. Cars that get over a hundred miles to the gallon, are street legal, get five-star crash ratings, go 140 miles per hour, and that you can buy for less than the cost of a Camry. WIKISPEED is still constantly improving the vehicle, but if you want to buy one, deposit twenty-five grand at wikispeed.com, and they'll get you a car in three months. And they use Scrum to do it. They, like many of the best teams now, work in one-week Sprints. Every Thursday they sit down and look at the massive backlog of things they have to do, everything from prototyping a new dashboard design to testing turn signals. They've prioritized that list, and then they say, "Okay, given that list, how many things can we do this week?" And by "do" they mean "done"—done completely. These new features work. The car drives. Each week. Each Sprint.

Walking into Team WIKISPEED's lair north of Seattle on an average Thursday, you see the glorious organized chaos that is a machine shop. There are bins of tools and saws and electronics and fasteners and wrenches. A CNC router sits in a corner next to the half-constructed frame of a car in bay three. A drill press and metal bender sit off to one side like puppies eager to be played with. Above the frame on the day we visit is a picture of the person who's buying the car—Tim Myer. He likes mountain climbing and chips and cider. He doesn't like not knowing what's going on or not having options. You can find him in the hills on weekends and square dancing at the Tractor every other Monday night.

In front, in bay one, sits the first car Team WIKISPEED made—the car that participated in a ten-million-dollar XPrize contest for cars achieving a fuel efficiency of 100 mpg. Team WIKISPEED came in tenth, beating out more than a hundred competitors from big auto companies and universities. As a result, they were invited to the 2011 Detroit Auto Show and were put right in front, between Chevy and Ford. This car is now their test bed for new ideas.

Next to the car is a twelve-foot-high wall of whiteboard stretching the width of the shop. On it are dozens and dozens of one of the most common artifacts found in Scrum: sticky notes. On each of these brightly colored Post-its is a thing to be done: "drill tube for modular steering rack" . . . "prepare interior mold" . . . "install inner fender liners to prevent splash from tires," etc.

The board is divided into a few columns: Backlog . . . Doing . . . Done. Each Sprint, Team WIKISPEED's members put into the Backlog column as many Post-its as they think can get done that week. As the week goes by, a member of the team will take up one of those tasks and move the sticky to Doing. When it's finished, it'll get moved to Done. Everyone on the team can see what everyone else is working on at every moment.

An important point: nothing gets moved to Done unless it can be used by the customer. In other words, you can *drive* the car. And if someone drives the car and says, "Hey, the turn signals are sticking," that problem is dealt with in the next Sprint.

Sprints are what are often called "time boxes." They're of a set duration. You don't do a one-week Sprint and then a three-week Sprint. You have to be consistent. You want to establish a work rhythm where people know how much they can get done in a set period of time. Often that quantity surprises them.

One crucial element of an individual Sprint, though, is that once the team commits to what they're going to accomplish, the tasks are locked in. Nothing else can be added by anyone outside the team. Later, I'll get further into the reasons why, but for now just know that interfering and distracting the team slows its speed dramatically.

As I mentioned, in the first Scrum we were running four-week Sprints. Near the end of the first Sprint we felt we weren't going fast enough—that we could do more. We looked at videos of the All Blacks doing the *haka* and breaking through opposing lines. *Why aren't we like that?* we asked ourselves. *Why don't we have that kind of spirit?* Our goal was not just to be a good team, but the best. How could we do that? Once again, the answer turned out to be something simple that we stole from someone else—the daily meeting.

Daily Stand-Up

Outside a city I can't name, in a company I can't mention, a group of people gathers every day to ponder how to put other people into space. Since rocket ships are really intercontinental ballistic missiles with a human payload, there is a certain amount of security and secrecy in the private space-travel effort. And it *is* a business, not merely a billionaire's pipe dream. As I write, another private rocket just docked with the International Space Station for the second time. Even the US government doesn't have that capability at the moment.

But in this particular building, on this particular day, these particular people are wrestling with how big the box should be that holds the rocket's avionics package. Avionics tell the rocket where it is, where it's going, and how to get there. Think of it as the rocket ship's mind.

There are two teams: one hardware and one software, each composed of about seven people. Every day each team gathers in front of a floor-to-ceiling whiteboard stretching from one end of the wall to the other. Just like at Team WIKISPEED there are a few columns drawn on the board: Backlog, Doing, Done. Listed in the columns are only the things that the team needs to get done in this Sprint. The tasks range from working with one of half a dozen specialty circuit-board vendors to mapping out how the accelerometer will talk to the rest of the ship. The Scrum Master, the person in charge of running the process, asks each team member three questions:

1. What did you do yesterday to help the team finish the Sprint?
2. What will you do today to help the team finish the Sprint?
3. What obstacles are getting in the team's way?

That's it. That's the whole meeting. If it takes more than fifteen minutes, you're doing it wrong. What this does is help the whole team know exactly where everything is in the Sprint. Are all the tasks going to be completed on time? Are there opportunities to help other team members overcome obstacles? There's no assigning of tasks from above—the team is autonomous; *they* do that. There's no detailed reporting to management. Anyone in management or on another team can walk by and look at the avionics Scrum board and know exactly where everything stands.

So when the first Scrum team wanted to figure out how they could be like the All Blacks, they went into the literature to find out how the best teams did it. One of the great things about software development is that the situation early on was so bad, and so much money was being wasted—billions and billions each year—that people spent a lot of time studying why, and there was data on everything.

One of the people who spent years looking at how things are made in the software business was Jim Coplien at AT&T's legendary Bell Labs. Coplien, who is referred to both by himself and others as "The Cope," spent years looking at hundreds of software projects, trying to figure out why a small minority went well while the majority were disasters. In the early 1990s he was invited to look at a project at Borland Software Corporation that was making a new spreadsheet product called "Quattro Pro for Windows." For the project, one million lines of software code had been created. They took thirty-one months to produce and were the output of eight people. That means each team member produced one thousand lines of code each week. That's the fastest of any team on record, and Jim wanted to know how they did it.

What he did was map all the communication flows within the team—who was talking to whom, where information was flowing, and where it wasn't. This type of mapping is a tool that can be used to spot bottlenecks or information hoarders. The greater the communication saturation—the more everyone knows everything—the faster the team. Basically, the metric spun off by this type of analysis measures how well everyone knows what they need to get their work done. Borland had the highest rating ever: 90 percent. Most companies hover around 20 percent.

So how could we get that kind of saturation on our team? The thing that cripples communication saturation is specialization—the number of roles and titles in a group. If people have a special title, they tend to do only things that seem a match for that title. And to protect the power of that role, they tend to hold on to specific knowledge.

So we got rid of all titles. I called everyone in and told them to rip up their business cards. If someone wanted to put a title on their resume, they could do it for external use only. In here, where the work was done, there were only team members.

The other ingredient in the Borland team's "secret sauce" was that they would have everyone on the team meet every single day to discuss how they were performing. Getting everyone together in a room was key, because it gave the team the opportunity to self-organize around challenges. If someone was stuck with a problem—if the accelerometer wasn't talking to the altimeter—everyone saw that the impediment could block the whole Sprint, and they swarmed on it, making sure it got fixed pronto.

At Borland the daily meeting was an hour at least. That struck me as too long, so I looked at the core things that need to be communicated in that huddle and came up with the three questions.

And that's how the daily meeting came to operate. We had certain rules. The meeting was held at the same time every day, and *everyone* had to be there. If the entire team wasn't present, communication simply didn't happen. And it didn't matter what time of day the meeting took place, as long as it was at the same time every day. The point was to give the team a regular heartbeat.

The second rule was that the meeting couldn't last more than fifteen minutes. We wanted it to be crisp, direct, and to the point. If something required further discussion, we noted it and met further after the daily meeting. The idea was to get the most actionable and valuable information in the least amount of time.

The third rule was that everyone had to actively participate. To help this happen, I said that everyone had to stand up. That way there'd be active talking and listening going on. It also would keep the meetings short.

This is the reason such a meeting is often called the Daily Stand-up or Daily Scrum. It doesn't really matter *what* you call it. It has to be at the same time every day, with the same three questions, with everyone standing up, and last no more than fifteen minutes.

The problem that I frequently see crop up is that people have a tendency to treat the Daily Stand-up as simply individual reporting. "I did this . . . I'll do that"—then on to the next person. The more optimum approach is closer to a football huddle. A wide receiver might say, "I'm having a problem with that defensive lineman," to which an offensive blocker might respond, "I'll take care of that. I'll open that line." Or the quarterback might say, "Our running game is hitting a wall; let's surprise them with a pass to the left." The idea is for the team to quickly confer on how to move toward victory— i.e., complete the Sprint. Passivity is not only lazy, it actively hurts the rest of the team's performance. Once spotted, it needs to be eliminated immediately.

I want aggressive teams—ones that come out of the daily meeting knowing the most important thing they need to accomplish that day. One person will hear another say that a task will take a day, but another team member might know how to do it in an hour if they work together. I want teams emerging from that meeting saying things like, "Let's nail this. Let's do this." The team needs to *want* to be great.

My standard speech to teams large and small is: "Do you really want to suck forever? Is that what your motivation is in life? Because it's a choice, you know—you don't *have* to be that way." A team has to demand greatness from itself.

At Easel, with the first Scrum team, we implemented the Daily Stand-up during the third Sprint. We'd planned out four weeks of work for that Sprint—pretty much the same workload as the previous month. We finished it all in a week. A 400-percent improvement. That first Friday the whole team just looked around at one another and said, "Wow." That's when I knew I might be on to something.

Time and Time Again

That kind of improvement was baked into Scrum from that third Sprint. It's the design goal of Scrum. In certain cases I've seen highly disciplined teams increase their productivity eight times. That's what makes Scrum so revolutionary. You can get more stuff done faster and cheaper—twice the work in half the time. And remember, it's not just in business that time is important. Time makes up your life, so wasting it is actually a slow form of suicide.

What Scrum does is alter the very way you think about time. After engaging for a while in Sprints and Stand-ups, you stop seeing time as a linear arrow into the future but, rather, as something that is fundamentally cyclical. Each Sprint is an opportunity to do something totally new; each day, a chance to improve. Scrum encourages a holistic worldview. The person who commits to it will value each moment as a returning cycle of breath and life.

I've always been dismayed by how long house-remodeling jobs can take. My wife and I used to remind each other, it'll take twice as long and cost twice as much as we think. And that's if we were lucky. I'm sure you've heard the same horror stories as I: the kitchen job that was supposed to take two weeks that ended up taking six, leaving the family eating takeout for more than a month; the electrical work that exceeded the estimate by three times; the minor job that just seemed to take forever to get done. Well, a couple of years ago my friend and fellow Agile thinker Eelco Rustenburg told me at dinner that he'd decided to redo his house—the whole thing, soup to nuts. He'd be tackling all the rooms, installing new wiring, putting in new appliances, slapping a fresh coat of paint on everything. And it was only going to take six weeks.

We all laughed and began to regale Eelco with *our* remodeling tales of woe. "Six weeks for a whole house?" I said, laughing. "Not going to happen. It took six weeks to redo my *kitchen,* though they promised me two. You'll be living in a hotel for the rest of the year."

"Nope," he said. "It's going to be on time and on budget. I'm going to do it using Scrum."

Now, *that* got me excited—the idea of using Scrum in a completely different arena than software. I ran into Eelco about six months later and asked him how it had gone. "Great," he said. "Six weeks to the day. Now my *neighbor,* that's another story."

Here's what happened. Eelco decided to make the contractors work as a Scrum team. He had weekly projects they had to move to Done, and in the contractor's trailer parked in his front lawn he had a Scrum board full of sticky notes listing out tasks. Every morning he'd gather the carpenters, the electricians, the plumbers, or whoever else was needed for that week's Sprint and go over what was done the day before, what they were going to get done today, and what was getting in their way.

Eelco says it made them think and communicate about the project in a different way than they had before. Plumbers and carpenters talked about how they could help one another work faster. Shortages of materials were discovered before their absence stopped all progress. But he said the main thing the Stand-ups did was remove dependencies. On any construction project a lot of time is spent waiting for one part of the job to be done before the next can begin, and often these phases involve different skill sets— electrical installation and drywall hanging, for instance. What the

Daily Stand-up meeting did was get all these people into a room where they quickly figured out how they could work together as a team. They were no longer simply individuals with separate skills but, rather, a team trying to move a house to Done.

And it worked. Six weeks later the project was completed. Eelco and his family moved back in. Life was good. When he told me this, I was surprised, but I congratulated him on having some great contractors. But wait, he told me, that's not the whole story. Down the block from his house a neighbor wanted to do almost exactly the same work on *his* house. They both lived in an old part of the Netherlands, and their houses had been built at exactly the same time, to exactly the same plan. The neighbor saw what a great job the contractors had done on Eelco's place and figured he'd repeat the magic.

The same workers were hired, but this time it took them *three months*. Same people. Same kind of house. Same job. Twice the time and, of course, twice the money. The only difference was that the neighbor didn't use Scrum. The problems that Scrum forces to the surface weren't discovered until too late. People didn't coordinate in the same way and were forced to wait for someone else to be done to begin their work. Eelco's neighbor ended up paying nearly twice as much as Eelco, most of that to people waiting for someone else to get *their* job done.

Think about your job. How much of your time is wasted while you're waiting for someone else to finish their work, or for information to be delivered, or because you're trying to do too many things at once? Maybe *you* would rather be at work all day—*me,* I'd rather be surfing.

SCRUM

THE TAKEAWAY

Time Is Finite. Treat It That Way. Break down your work into what can be accomplished in a regular, set, short period—optimally one to four weeks. And if you've caught the Scrum fever, call it a Sprint.

Demo or Die. At the end of each Sprint, have something that's *done*— something that can be used (to fly, drive, whatever).

Throw Away Your Business Cards. Titles are specialized status markers. Be known for what you *do,* not how you're referred to.

Everyone Knows Everything. Communication saturation accelerates work.

One Meeting a Day. When it comes to team check-ins, once a day is enough. Get together for fifteen minutes at the Daily Stand-up, see what can be done to increase speed, and do it.

CHAPTER FIVE

Waste Is a Crime

The heart of Scrum is rhythm. Rhythm is deeply important to human beings. Its beat is heard in the thrumming of our blood and rooted in some of the deepest recesses of our brains. We're pattern seekers, driven to seek out rhythm in all aspects of our lives.

However, the patterns we seek aren't necessarily rewarding or optimized to bring us happiness. For example, there are the negative rhythms of the addict and the depressed. You can walk the halls of just about any office building and see these negative patterns made manifest. They're likely to be found anywhere that someone feels frustrated at being stymied, or quietly desperate as it dawns on them that they're trapped in an uncaring system, or angry at being viewed as a cog in a machine.

This is part of the human experience. You can go back thousands of years and read the writings of other people, just like us, whose lives were caught up in a system they felt helpless against. But we seem to have mastered that trapped feeling sometime during the twentieth century. Throughout the business environment especially, we created an acute depersonalization that seems dictated by fate.

What Scrum does is create a different kind of pattern. It accepts that we're habit-driven creatures, seekers of rhythm, somewhat predictable, but also somewhat magical and capable of greatness. When I created Scrum, I thought, *What if I can take human patterns and make them positive rather than negative? What if I can design a virtuous, self-reinforcing cycle that encourages the best parts of ourselves and diminishes the worst?* In giving Scrum a daily and weekly rhythm, I guess what I was striving for was to offer people the chance to *like* the person they see in the mirror.

But there are pitfalls. What look like virtuous patterns can end up being nothing but folly—nothing but waste. That's what I'm going to spend this chapter talking about: the waste that infects our work, the cancer that eats at our productivity, our organizations, our lives, and our society.

The other day I was interviewing someone for a job at Scrum, Inc., and I asked why he wanted to work in a Scrum company. He told me a story. He worked at a company that put out textbooks and ancillary products like workbooks, course materials, presentations, etc. His job was to identify leading scholars in a particular field and work with them to produce these products. In a way it was exciting. He was a history major, a scholar of the American Colonial period, and he had a chance to work with some of the leading minds in his field.

"I worked for a year," he said. "A year spent developing dozens of different products. At the end of the year, we reviewed for the first time what we'd accomplished. And fully half of the work I'd done over the past year was thrown away. Not because it wasn't good, but because the market wasn't there, or direction had changed. Six months of my life were completely and totally wasted."

At that point a certain indignation and anger crept into his voice. And then determination. "I hope that Scrum won't let that happen, that my work will have purpose, that what I do will actually matter."

You might think that an extreme example. Fifty-percent waste. But it's actually pretty good. When I go into a company I usually find that about 85 percent of effort is wasted. Only a sixth of any of the work done actually produces something of value. Deep within ourselves, as we repeat the rhythm of our days, we know that's true. That's why we all laugh, a bit nervously, at jokes about the inherent insanity and wastefulness of life in a modern corporation.

I'm here to tell you that it shouldn't be funny. It should be shameful. We should mourn the lives and potential we're wasting. I briefly introduced Toyota's Taiichi Ohno in the first chapter of this book, where he said, "Waste is a crime against society more than a business loss." His thoughts about waste deeply influenced mine, and I want to spend some time talking about them.

Ohno talked about three different types of waste. He used the Japanese words: *Muri,* waste through unreasonableness; *Mura,* waste through inconsistency; and *Muda,* waste through outcomes. These ideas are highly aligned with Deming's PDCA cycle, which I wrote about earlier: **Plan, Do,** Check, **Act. Plan** means avoid *Muri.* **Do** means avoid *Mura.* **Check** means avoid *Muda.* **Act** means the will, motivation, and determination to do all that. I'm going to go through these steps one at a time and point out what to avoid— from waste in inventory, to the waste of not doing it right the first time, to the waste of working too hard, to the emotional waste of unreasonable expectations.[1]

Do One Thing at a Time

I often hear people brag about their ability to multitask. I'm sure you do too. If you don't crow about it yourself, you know someone who does—the guy who does three projects at once, who drives and talks on his cell phone, who promotes his competence by complaining loudly about all the things he has to juggle every day. This sort of "busy-brag" is becoming part of our work culture. In job descriptions you now see requirements like "must be able to balance five projects simultaneously."

The ability to juggle seems so *attractive*—especially in an age in which information is flowing through a thousand different pipelines and "must do nows" are proliferating. We want to be *that* guy—the Super-Juggler. We tell ourselves we can. Unfortunately, we *can't*. And the more we think we can, the worse we actually are at it.

An especially apt example is that daily practice of multitasking: driving and talking on a cell phone. The research is very clear on this. People who drive while talking on cell phones—even the hands-free variety—get into more accidents than people who don't. The problem is especially alarming when you consider that, according to the National Highway Transportation Safety Administration, at any given moment 8 percent of people on the road are talking on a cell phone.

That is what multitasking has bequeathed us.

Here's a quote from my favorite paper on the subject:

> . . . even when participants direct their gaze at objects in the driving environment, they often fail to "see" them when they are talking on a cell phone because attention has been directed away from the external environment and toward an internal, cognitive context associated with the phone conversation.[2]

That's right, people will actually look at an object, the car they're about to rear-end, or the tree they're about to wrap their car around, and *not see it*. And yet, we persist in driving and talking on the phone.

I can read your mind right now. You're thinking, *Well, other people can't do it. But me, I'm a high-powered executive"* or *"I'm smart. I can do it; they can't."* The literature is pretty clear on the topic, though: if you think you're good at it, you're actually worse than everyone else. The University of Utah, which has done a lot of interesting research in this area, asked people whether they thought they were good at multitasking activities such as using a cell phone while driving, and then they tested them to see if they were right. The researchers' conclusions:

> Perceptions of the ability to multi-task were found to be badly inflated; in fact, the majority of participants judged themselves to be above average in the ability to multi-task. These estimations had little grounding in reality. Thus, it appears that the people who are most likely to multi-task and most apt to use a cell phone while driving are those with the most inflated views of their abilities.[3]

The lead author of the study, David Sanbonmatsu, told the NPR blog *Shots* in January of 2013, "People don't multitask because they're good at it. They do it because they are more distracted. They have trouble inhibiting the impulse to do another activity." In other words, the people who multitask the most just *can't* focus. They can't help themselves.

I probably shouldn't say "they." I should say "we." We all do it. It's hard not to. The key thing to remember is that it's stupid. I want you to do a little exercise. It's one that I have people do all the time in my training courses. It's simple, but it shows the deep impact of focus and flow. It shows just how painful multitasking is to your brain, and how much it slows you down even when you think it speeds you up. It demonstrates just how *wasteful* it is.

Here's what I want you to do. The task is to write down the numbers 1–10, the Roman numerals 1–10 (I, II, III, IV, etc.), and the letters A–L. Time yourself doing this. You want to do it as fast as possible. But here's how I want you to do it the first time. Write the Arabic numeral, the Roman numeral, then the letter, so your piece of paper looks like this:

1	*I*	*A*
2	*II*	*B*
3	*III*	*C*

You're doing each row at a time. Time yourself. I'll do it right now with you. Took me thirty-nine seconds. Now, instead of doing it by rows, do it by columns. So first you'll do all the Arabic numerals, then the Roman, then the letters. I'll do it too. Nineteen seconds. Simply by doing tasks one at a time, instead of switching from one context to another, I halved the amount of time it took me.

Okay, Sutherland, I hear you saying, *that's all well and good for talking on the cell phone and making silly lists, but I run a business. I have to do a bunch of things at once—have my teams address five projects simultaneously. I have to remain competitive. I can't afford not to.*

Here's where the incredible amount of research done on software projects comes in handy again. Remember, people have done this research because they kept wasting hundreds of millions of dollars every year, and their products just got worse. And so, being the engineers they are, they started looking at the data and measuring everything. There's a great chart that appears in one of the classic works on how to develop computer software, *Quality Software Management* by Gerald Weinberg:[4]

Number of Simultaneous Projects	Percent of Time Available per Project	Loss to Context Switching
1	100%	0%
2	40%	20%
3	20%	40%
4	10%	60%
5	5%	75%

The "Loss to Context Switching" column is pure waste. That's right: if you have five projects, a full 75 percent of your work goes nowhere—three-quarters of your day is flushed down the toilet. It's why you couldn't write the rows and columns at the same speed. It's a result of the physical limitations of your brain.

A scientist named Harold Pashler demonstrated this in the early 1990s. He called it "Dual Task Interference." He conducted a few simple experiments. He would have one group do one really simple thing, say press a button if a light went on. And then he'd give another group that task plus another simple one, like pressing a different button depending on the *color* of the flashing light. As soon as another task was added, no matter how simple, the time involved doubled. Pashler theorized that there was some sort of processing bottleneck—that people can really only think about one thing at a time. He reckoned that a certain amount of effort is involved in "packing up" one process, reaching into your memory and pulling out another, and then running that job. And each time you switch tasks, that process takes time.[5]

As a result, you don't do it. You concentrate fully on one thing at a time. You talk on the cell phone, and even though all you're discussing is picking up milk, you literally can't see the car in front of you. Your brain can't process those two things at the same time. There has been some recent research using fMRIs to map the brain as it's actually thinking. The data show that it's possible to think about two things at once only with one process running in each lobe of your brain. But even then, the scans indicate that the thinking isn't happening simultaneously but, rather, the brain is switching from one task to another in serial fashion. Basically, there's a control function, so you can't argue with yourself too vigorously.[6]

So back to work. What does this mean when you're trying to get things done? Well, let's look at a typical team. This year they've decided to do three projects. Let's call them A, B, and C. And they plan out their year, saying they'll do a little bit on this project, then that one, and then the next one, so their calendar looks like what's shown on page 93.

By trying to do everything at once—the classic strategy—completing those three projects will take them till the end of July. But by approaching the aggregate in a Scrum fashion, by driving each project to Done one at a time, they minimize the cost of context switching. They're able to finish by the beginning of May.

They don't change how big the project is, or what's involved in creating it, but just by doing one thing *exclusively* before moving on, the work takes a little more than half as much time. *Half.*

And the other half? That's pure waste. Not a thing more is produced. Not a dollar saved. Not a new innovation implemented. It is just a waste of human life. It's working for no purpose.

PRIORITIZING BETWEEN PROJECTS

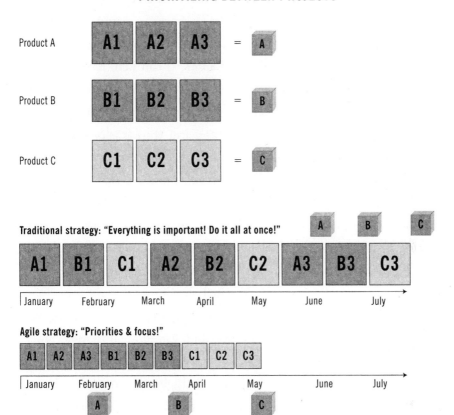

So that's the cost of multitasking. We all live in a world where there are multiple demands on our time. People want different things from us: the phone rings with a really important call, the kids arrive home from school, the boss walks into our office. What I want you to do, though, is be *conscious* of the cost of context switching. It's very real, and you should try to minimize it.

If you're working with something complicated—for example, writing a report, creating a presentation, developing a piece of software, or crafting a book, you're holding an incredibly complex object in your mind. You must take into account dozens of factors, remember what you've done, where you want to go, and what the impediments might be. That's a pretty tricky thing to do. And what happens if you're interrupted or have to switch quickly to another project, even just for a moment? You guessed it: that carefully built mental architecture collapses. It can take *hours* of work just to get back to the same state of awareness. That's the cost. So minimize that waste by trying to do *all at once* those tasks that require a specific kind of concentration. Put those tasks into blocks of time where it's possible to shut off your phone and put up a "Do not disturb!" sign.

Some research has actually been done that shows that multitasking not only wastes your time but makes you stupid. A study done at the University of London back in 2005[7] (admittedly, a very small non-peer-reviewed study, but still) measured how stupid multitasking can make you. Psychiatrist Glenn Wilson took four men and four women and tested their IQ under quiet conditions and distracting conditions (phones ringing, e-mail arriving). During the tests he measured the subjects' skin conductance, heart rate, and blood pressure. And, interestingly, the mean IQ scores of the subjects dropped by more than ten points when in distracting environments. Even more interesting, the drop-off was worse for men than women. (Perhaps, for some reason, women are more habituated to distraction.)

Half Done Isn't Done at All

As I've mentioned, Scrum takes a lot of its thinking from the Japanese manufacturing model that was codified in the classic book *Toyota Production System* by Taiichi Ohno. In the United States this model has been interpreted as "Lean" manufacturing. Basically, the idea is to eliminate as much waste as possible on the factory floor. Now, most of us aren't looking to improve flow through an automobile plant, but some of the ideas are applicable to any kind of work at all.

One idea I want to address here is called "Work in Process," or sometimes just "inventory." The idea is that it's wasteful to have a bunch of stuff lying around that isn't being used to build something. That stuff, whether it be car doors or widgets, actually costs money, and if it's sitting around on the factory floor, it means that huge amounts of money are bound up in inventory that isn't actually needed right then. This changes how you look at things that are *in process*. If, for example, all an auto company has is a bunch of half-built cars, it has expended a lot of money and effort but hasn't created anything of real value. In Lean manufacturing, the idea is to minimize the amount of half-built stuff lying around.

The power of that idea applies to every type of work. Let's take something very simple that nearly every married adult on the planet has: the "honey-do" list. In any given week, my list usually has on it ten to twenty chores that I need to take care of. They range from repainting the bathroom to picking up more dog food, from paying the mortgage to raking leaves. This is the stuff of daily life, the friction of being a fully integrated member of society. Now, there are a bunch of different ways of attacking that list. But the biggest mistake you can make is to try to do five things at once. That's multitasking, and you probably won't get all of them done, which leaves you with work in process.

Imagine (or, if you're unfortunate, remember) having five tasks *partially* done. You've painted one wall of the bathroom, the dog food is still in the trunk, the mortgage check has been written but not mailed, and the leaves are piled up but not bagged. You've expended effort but haven't created any value. The value arrives when the drop cloths and paint cans are out of the bathroom, the dog has been fed, the bank gets its money, and the yard is actually clear of leaves. Doing half of something is, essentially, doing nothing.

As I've said, in Scrum there is a rhythm to the work. Every iteration, or Sprint, the team tries to get a number of things done. But that "Done" implies a complete, deliverable product that can be used by a customer. If something is half done at the end of the Sprint, you're worse off than if you hadn't started at all. You've expended resources, effort, and time and gotten nothing to a deliverable state. You have a half-constructed car. It might have been better to create something smaller—something that really works.

Another way to look at work in process or inventory is simply as physical inventory. Let's take cars, for example. Having tons of cars sitting on a lot unsold is a problem for an automaker. But not having cars available to be sold is also a problem. So each automaker and dealership operation engages in a careful balancing act. They want to produce just enough vehicles to keep stock available, but not so many that they've invested huge amounts of money in things that aren't selling.

Let me put some actual numbers to that. In December of 2012, General Motors started laying off people in some of its auto plants in America. Why? The company had built too many cars. At the end of November that year they had 245,853 full-size pickups sitting in car lots across the country. That represented 139 days' worth of trucks. At average pricing, those unsold vehicles represented about $7.5 billion. That's billion with a *b*. All that money, in this case truck-shaped money, but money nonetheless, sitting there unsold. So they started shuttering plants, putting people out of work right before Christmas.

How many days of inventory *should* a car company work toward? The industry standard is about sixty days—less than half what GM had. Think about it. When you pick up dog food at the store, you don't want to purchase a six-month supply. It takes up space in the garage and might cost so much money so that the mortgage check won't be able to go out that month.

Now, you might think, hey, they've *built* the cars; they've got that part done, right? They aren't *half-built* cars—what's the problem? The problem is that too much inventory is pretty much the same thing as work in process. If you're tying up a huge amount of value in things that aren't *delivering* value, you won't have those resources to do other things—such as market more, or push more sales, or explore new ideas. You have to have *some* inventory; the key is to minimize it.

Jobs that aren't done and products that aren't being used are two aspects of the same thing: invested effort with no positive outcome. Don't do it.

Do It Right the First Time

Dr. James Womack, the founder of the Lean Enterprise Institute at MIT and the author of a bunch of different books on Lean manufacturing, tells a wonderful story about the perils of "re-work" in his classic *The Machine That Changed the World.* Jim and his team spent years traveling the world looking at the biggest manufacturing effort ever undertaken by humans: making cars. He wanted to figure out why some companies made cars faster and with fewer defects than other companies. By now, any rational manufacturer uses what Jim decided to call Lean manufacturing, but back then things were different.

97

One of the biggest differences between manufacturers was in the luxury-car market. In Japan, such companies as Toyota, Honda, and Nissan spent an average of 16.8 hours making a luxury car. Parts went in at one end of the factory, and, about 17 hours later, a Lexus emerged. And they had 34 defects per hundred vehicles. Not bad.

In Europe, though, the story was different. Such companies as Mercedes-Benz, Audi, and BMW took 57 hours to make a car, and they had 78.7 defects for every hundred vehicles.

Why did it take the Europeans so long? And why so many defects? BMW isn't exactly known for making crappy cars. Here's why: In a Toyota plant when a problem shows up on the line, every worker has the ability to stop the whole line. When that happens, everyone swarms around where the line stopped—not to yell at the guy for stopping the line, but to fix whatever problem is there. They don't want any cars coming out the other end with things that have to be fixed. They fix the problem once, and it's solved forever. If they don't, that same defect could go into hundreds of vehicles.

At European luxury-car makers there was a different way of doing things. At the end of the production line were dozens of people in white lab coats going around fixing all the problems. They made sure the car door had that BMW *clunk* when the door closed, or the engine purred with exactly the right tone. They made sure all the parts meshed together properly. They viewed themselves not as manufacturers but as craftsmen, artisans making a thing of beauty. That's great when you're making a few cars, but when you're making millions, those costs add up. As Womack reports in his book:

> . . . the German plant was expending more effort to fix the problems it had just created than the Japanese plant required to make a nearly perfect car the first time.[8]

You read that right. The Germans spent more time fixing a car they'd just made than the Japanese did making one in the first place. There's a reason Toyota became the number one car manufacturer on the planet. They did it right the first time.

But we don't always do things perfectly the first time. We're human; we make mistakes. How you deal with those mistakes can have an extraordinary impact on how fast you can get things done, and at what level of quality. At Toyota, as I said, every worker in the factory can stop the line. The idea is that the process is being continuously improved, and that the right moment to fix a problem is when it is observed, not after the fact.

A few years ago I was in California talking to the development people at Palm. They made some of the first of what were then called Personal Digital Assistants (PDAs), which we now call cell phones. They tracked everything they did automatically. One of the many things they measured was how long it took to fix a bug—that is, how much time it took a software developer to fix a problem he'd introduced into the system. The computer tracked this automatically, each and every time.

So let's say that one day, when the testers tried to integrate Matt's code into the rest of the system, they detected a bug. Matt, like most software developers, wouldn't want to go back and fix that code right away. Instead, he'd vow to get to it later. First, he'd write *new* code.

At most companies this kind of testing doesn't even happen on the same day. It could be weeks or months before all the code is tested, and only then are the problems discovered. But Palm performed daily, automated tests of all their code, so they knew right away when there was a problem.

They looked at the "Matts" across the entire company—hundreds of developers—and they decided to analyze how long it took to fix a bug if they did it right away versus if they tried to fix it a few weeks later. Now, remember, software can be a pretty complicated and involved thing, so what do you think was the difference?

It took twenty-four times longer. If a bug was addressed on the day it was created, it would take an hour to fix; three weeks later, it would take *twenty-four* hours. It didn't even matter if the bug was big or small, complicated or simple—it always took twenty-four times longer three weeks later. As you can imagine, every software developer in the company was soon required to test and fix their code on the same day.

The human mind has limits. We can only remember so many things; we can really only concentrate on one thing at a time. This tendency—for the process of fixing things to get harder as more time elapses—represents a similar limitation. When you're working on a project, there's a whole mind space that you create around it. You know all the different reasons *why* something is being done. You're holding a pretty complicated construct in your head. Re-creating that construct a week later is *hard*. You have to remember all the factors that you were considering when you made that choice. You have to re-create the thought process that led you to that decision. You have to become your past self again, put yourself back inside a mind that no longer exists. Doing that takes time. A *long* time. Twenty-four times as long as it would take if you had fixed the problem when you first discovered it.

I'm sure you've had this experience yourself in your own work, and the lesson is one you were probably taught as a child: *Do things right the first time.* The only thing the data now adds is that if you do make a mistake—and we all make them—fix it as soon as you notice it. If you don't, you'll pay for it.

Working Too Hard Makes More Work

When Scott Maxwell, the founder of the venture capital firm Open-View Venture Partners, was working as a consultant at McKinsey & Company in the early 1990s, he received what he considered to be an odd pep talk. Jon Katzenbach, then a director at the company and now the author of several books and head of the Katzenbach Center at Booz Allen Hamilton, gave Scott some advice he never forgot. Jon said that back in the seventies, when he was starting out, everyone worked seven days a week at McKinsey. That was the culture; that was what was expected. If you didn't work that many hours, you were seen as not pulling your weight, not contributing to the team.

For religious reasons Jon worked only six days a week. And he noticed something. While he was working fewer hours, he was actually getting *more* done than the guys—and they were almost all guys back then—working every single day. Then he decided to try only five days a week. And he found that he was getting even more done. Work too long, he said, and you get less done. He told Scott that he always wanted to drop down to four or even three days a week to see what would happen, but he wasn't sure that the company would accept it.

Scott and the other young consultants scoffed at the idea at the time. *Work fewer hours? Isn't that slacking off?* But the idea stayed with Scott for years as he moved through his career, and as CEO and founder of OpenView Venture Partners he started investing in technology companies, some of which were doing Scrum. He heard that I'd invented Scrum and lived in the same city, so he invited me to breakfast one morning. Over coffee and croissants, Scott told me the story of one of the companies in which he'd invested where the development teams had implemented Scrum and how they'd improved their productivity 25 to 35 percent. He was really impressed. My instant response: "Twenty-five to thirty-five percent? They must be doing it wrong!!!"

Scott decided to bring Scrum to OpenView and implement it throughout the company. The investment guys, the research folk, senior management, the admin staff—everyone was put on a Scrum team. And eventually something happened that is one of the great things about Scrum—OpenView discovered how people *actually* work instead of how they *say* they work.

At that time OpenView was like a lot of high-powered offices. Ingrained in the corporate culture was the expectation that people would work late and on the weekends. These were aggressive, ambitious people. But they were getting burned out, depressed, and demoralized. It was such a tough environment that some people couldn't take it and quit.

But as the firm's teams started working with Scrum, Scott noticed a shift in productivity. Working more hours stopped producing more output. He pulled me into his office one day and drew this curve on a whiteboard (see page 103).

The y-axis is productivity, and the x-axis is hours of work. The peak of productivity actually falls at a little bit less than forty hours a week. Armed with this data, Scott started to send people home early.

"It took them a while to get that I was serious," says Scott. "But eventually they came around to my way of thinking."

He started telling people that working late wasn't a sign of commitment; it was a sign of failure. "It's not because I want you to have a balanced life," he told people. "It's because you'll get more stuff done."

So no more nights, no more weekends. When people go on

DOUBLE OUTPUT BY CUTTING WORKLOAD

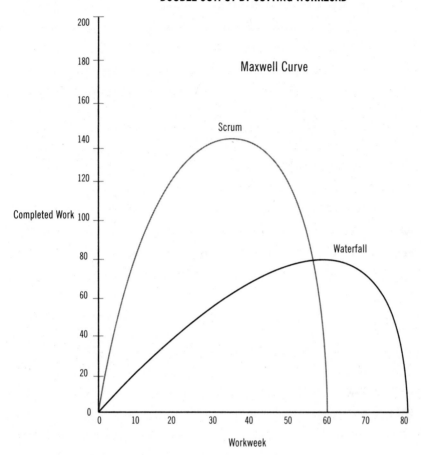

vacation, they are expected to go on vacation, not check e-mail, not check in with the office. If you can't actually take time off without having to make sure everything is going right at the office, the thinking goes, you aren't managing your teams well.

"A lot of companies don't practice [work-hour limits]," says Scott. "But there is a direct correlation. You get more done. You are happier. And you have higher quality." It's a no-brainer. Working less helps you get more done with higher quality.

Scott says the curve is different for different people, even for the same person at different times in their lives. "I've noticed as I've gotten older and in different roles that the peak output for me is at a lower number of hours than it was twenty years ago," he says. Physical fitness, diet, personal issues, and other factors all play a role, he thinks. But he also believes that his output reaches its peak faster as he has grown and thought quite deeply about how to work. "I've been able to attack more and more important-impact opportunities."

Why *is* it that if you work fewer hours, you get more done? It doesn't really seem to make sense on the face of it. Scott says that people who work too many hours start making mistakes, which, as we've seen, can actually take more effort to fix than to create. Overworked employees get more distracted and begin distracting others. Soon they're making bad decisions.

Jon Katzenbach's instincts were right. The disturbing evidence reveals that we have a very limited capability to make decisions, and the more energy-depleted we are, and the less downtime we get, the worse we are at it.

In April of 2011, a group of Israeli researchers published some remarkable research about decision making in the *Proceedings of the National Academy of Sciences of the United States of America*. Their paper, titled "Extraneous Factors in Judicial Decisions," looked at over a thousand judicial rulings by eight Israeli judges who presided over two different parole boards. The rulings covered Jewish-Israeli and Arab-Israeli criminals—both men and women. The crimes ranged from embezzlement and assault to murder and rape. The vast majority of the decisions the judges looked at were requests for parole.[9]

It seems fairly straightforward, right? These are esteemed judges using their years of experience and wisdom to make critical decisions affecting not only the lives of the prisoners and their victims but the well-being of the community as a whole. Each day they heard between fourteen and thirty-five cases.

So if you were a prisoner, what was the biggest factor in whether you'd go free or not? True remorse, perhaps? Your reformation and behavior in prison? The severity of your crime? None of those, actually. It turns out what *really* mattered was how long it had been since the judge had had a sandwich.

The researchers looked at what time judges made decisions, whether clemency was granted, and how long it had been since the judges had had a snack. If they'd just gotten to work, or back from a snack break, or back from lunch, they made favorable decisions more than 60 percent of the time. That rate dropped to nearly zero by the time of the next break.

Basically, right after a short break, judges came in with a more positive attitude and made more lenient decisions. They displayed more imagination and capacity to see that the world, and people, could change, could be different. But as they burned up their reserves of energy, they began to make more and more decisions that maintained the status quo.

I'm sure that if you asked these judges if they were certain they were making equally good decisions each time, they'd be affronted. But numbers, and sandwiches, don't lie. When we don't have any energy reserves left, we're prone to start making unsound decisions.

This phenomenon has been labeled "ego depletion." The idea is that making any choice involves an energy cost. It's an odd sort of exhaustion—you don't feel physically tired, but your capacity to make good decisions diminishes. What really changes is your self-control—your ability to be disciplined, thoughtful, and prescient.

A fascinating experiment shows just that. A group of researchers wanted to know how making decisions affects self-control. So they gathered the foot soldiers of psychological research—collegiate undergraduates—and had one set of them make a bunch of decisions. Specifically, these students were presented with different products and asked to choose which they preferred. They were told to think carefully because they'd be given a free gift at the end of the experiment, and their preferences would decide what they'd get. The other set of students had no decisions to make.[10]

The test group was asked questions, such as: What kind of scented candle do you like—vanilla or almond? What kind of shampoo brand do you prefer? Do you like this kind of candy or that? Then they were given the classic test of self-control: How long can you hold your hand in ice water?

Whatever resource is burned up by making decisions is also used up in self-regulation. The students who'd made all the product decisions simply couldn't hold their hands in the icy water as long as the control group that had been spared the decisions.

So there's a limited number of sound decisions you can make in any one day, and as you make more and more, you erode your ability to regulate your own behavior. You start making mistakes— eventually, serious ones. As the Maxwell Curve shows, those bad decisions impact productivity. So go home at five. Turn off the cell phone over the weekend. Watch a movie. Perhaps, most important, have a sandwich. By not working so much, you'll get more and better work done.

Scrum asks those who engage in it to break from the mindset of measuring merely hours. Hours themselves represent a cost. Instead, measure *output*. Who cares how many hours someone worked on something? All that matters is how fast it's delivered and how good it is.

Be Reasonable

There are three types of waste identified by Taiichi Ohno that lead to people working harder, and for more hours, than necessary. I've just pointed out why that's an incredibly bad idea, but recognizing these types of waste, which Ohno called *Muri,* or "Unreasonableness," is perhaps the most powerful lever for change we can reach.

The first is "Absurdity." You want to give your team challenging goals—to push them to reach for more. But you *don't* want them striving for absurd, impossible goals.

The second is "Unreasonable Expectations." How many times have you heard someone brag that through their own heroic efforts they saved a project? Usually this is greeted with backslaps, cheers, and congratulations. I see this as a fundamental flaw in the process. A team that depends on regular heroic actions to make its deadlines is not working the way it's supposed to work. Constantly moving from one crisis to the next causes burnout, and it doesn't allow for reasoned, continuous improvement. It's the difference between a cowboy riding in and rescuing the girl from the bad guys and a disciplined Marine platoon clearing the kill zone.

Ohno called the third type of waste "Overburden." It's the sort of behavior that Scott Adams regularly lampoons in his *Dilbert* cartoons. It includes onerous company policies that get in the way, unnecessary reporting that has people filling out forms for the sake of filling out forms, and meaningless meetings that suck up time and don't deliver any value.

While Ohno didn't mention a fourth type of waste, one comes to mind—i.e., "Emotional Waste." That type of waste is generated when a company has an asshole in its midst—someone who likes spinning up other people and putting them in a tizzy. Assholes often justify their behavior by claiming they're simply trying to make people work better. But they're merely indulging the negative aspects of their personality, and nothing is more undermining of a team's ability to excel.

Don't be an asshole—and don't allow, abet, or accept that behavior in others.

Flow

In a theoretically perfect world, there would be no process, no meetings, no forms, no reporting. Instead, there'd be the creation of *exactly* what the customer wants, even if the customer didn't know they wanted it yet. Any "process" that people use is wasteful, and that includes Scrum.

But we don't live in a perfect world, and bad processes are so ingrained in our thinking that, as an alternative, we need the lightest-weight process with the greatest impact on work. What Scrum does is focus us on trying to eliminate the pointless waste that seems part and parcel of work. I've tried to make it so that the process itself is the least disturbing framework you can have and still keep people focused.

What you really want in your work is effortless "flow." In the martial arts or in meditative practice, when you reach a sense of oneness with a motion, it is no longer an effort; it is energy effortlessly flowing through you. When you watch great dancers or singers, you sense that they're surrendering to a force greater than themselves as they let their art move through them. Reaching that spot in our work is what we should all seek.

But as the kung fu master, the monk, the dancer, or the opera star will all tell you, at the root of flow is discipline. There can be no wasted movement—nothing extraneous—just focused application of human capability. Waste is anything that distracts you from that. If you start thinking about work in terms of discipline and flow, you might just do something amazing.

THE TAKEAWAY

Multitasking Makes You Stupid. Doing more than one thing at a time makes you slower and worse at both tasks. *Don't do it.* If you think this doesn't apply to you, you're wrong—it does.

Half-Done Is Not Done. A half-built car simply ties up resources that could be used to create value or save money. Anything that's "in process" costs money and energy without delivering anything.

Do It Right the First Time. When you make a mistake, fix it right away. Stop everything else and address it. Fixing it later can take you more than twenty times longer than if you fix it now.

Working Too Hard Only Makes More Work. Working long hours doesn't get *more* done; it gets *less* done. Working too much results in fatigue, which leads to errors, which leads to having to fix the thing you just finished. Rather than work late or on the weekends, work weekdays only at a sustainable pace. And take a vacation.

Don't Be Unreasonable. Goals that are challenging are motivators; goals that are impossible are just depressing.

No Heroics. If you need a hero to get things done, you have a problem. Heroic effort should be viewed as a failure of planning.

Enough with the Stupid Policies. Any policy that *seems* ridiculous likely *is*. Stupid forms, stupid meetings, stupid approvals, stupid standards are just that—stupid. If your office seems like a *Dilbert* cartoon, fix it.

No Assholes. Don't be one, and don't allow the behavior. Anyone who causes emotional chaos, inspires fear or dread, or demeans or diminishes people needs to be stopped cold.

Strive for Flow. Choose the smoothest, most trouble-free way to get things done. Scrum is about enabling the most flow possible.

CHAPTER SIX

Plan Reality, Not Fantasy

"Hey, Jeff, we have a problem."

That's how a lot of my phone conversations start. People have backed themselves into a corner, and they pick up the phone and call me. This time it was Mark Landy, Medco's Chief Architect of Software. If you get your prescriptions through the mail, you more than likely deal with his company. At the time of this call Medco was a Fortune 100 firm with nearly $38 billion in revenue, the largest pharmaceutical company in the country, with tens of thousands of employees. And their management had just walked them off a cliff.

I got the call in December of 2006. That July, their president, Kenny Klepper, had announced to Wall Street his latest idea. Mark Landy described it this way: "We were trying to convince more and more people to switch to getting their prescriptions by mail. And there are some barriers to that." Barriers such as the appearance of inconvenience. But Mark said there were some ways around it. "Look, when you go into a pharmacy, your experience is minimally clinical. You hand over your prescription, sign a waiver saying you don't want to talk to the pharmacist, and walk out. We can improve that experience."

One of the things they wanted to do was put a pharmacist on the telephone with the patient—a pharmacist who was familiar not only with the drug being described, but with *all* the drugs being prescribed to that patient. The latter was particularly important if the patient had a chronic condition such as diabetes or heart disease, which 80 percent of the people on regular medication do. And most of those folks—certainly if they're older—are on six or more medications at the same time. And their doctors—specialists in different fields of health—don't always know it.

"Doctors don't [always] share information with each other. We, as the pharmacy, know more than the doctors know, and we know it in real time, [even] before the health insurance plan knows," said Landy.

So here was Klepper's idea: Let's create specialized pharmacies in five different sites spread across the country. There'll be the cardiac pharmacy, the diabetes pharmacy, the one for asthma, and so on. And we'll train pharmacists assigned to those sites to be aware of drug interactions, side effects, etc. And because the pharmacists will have comprehensive insight into the patient's condition, they'll be able to let doctors know when there might be contraindications. Let's say someone is diabetic. They're more likely to be overweight and, possibly, to have liver issues. As a result they'll metabolize drugs differently. So if a new doctor prescribes a blood pressure medication, the Medco pharmacist might call the doctor and recommend that he or she run a liver panel on the patient and adjust dosage if need be.

The goal was to bring new customers to Medco, which, for the most part, served companies and health insurance plans. By using these new pharmacies, or Therapeutic Resource Centers, customers could save money by cutting not necessarily their prescription costs but their overall medical costs, which rise when people either don't take their medications properly or take drugs that interact poorly with one another or with that person in particular. What's more, Medco would *guarantee* the cost savings. If a customer didn't save the amount of money Medco projected, Medco would pick up the difference.

Wall Street, to put it mildly, *liked* this notion. Pretty cool idea, right? Save money and provide better health care. More customers, more sales. Win-win. There was only one problem. While Klepper had checked with his managers that the idea was technically possible, he hadn't obtained details on how *long* this plan would take to implement. The people who would actually make it happen only found out about it after their president had promised Wall Street that the new system would be put in place on July 7, 2007. Come hell or high water.

Making that deadline was especially important to Medco, because while they'd been the first to start automated mail-order pharmacies, they weren't the only ones, and their competitors were hungry. Unfortunately, they had a lot of hurdles to leap. For example, much of the software the company relied on to direct their on-site robots was badly outdated. In Medco's five gargantuan plants filled with four thousand pharmacists processing prescriptions, robots whizzed about pulling pills while other robots handled packaging and mailing, and all those systems had to talk to one another with 100-percent accuracy, or someone could die.

The idea was that Klepper's brave new plan would give Medco a chance to update their aging systems and stay a step ahead of their competitors. It took the company nearly six months to figure out that they couldn't do it on time. Their calculations showed that, in the best-case scenario, they'd deliver the system at least one year late. Probably more. That's when they called me.

Why it took them *six months* to figure out that they couldn't do it in time is something that bears examination. It wasn't that they weren't smart, or didn't have the right teams in place, or even the right technology. It wasn't that they weren't working hard or being competitive. You don't get to be the biggest company in your sector without doing all that.

It was because they made a very basic mistake. They thought they could plan everything ahead of time. They spent months of effort making the sort of detailed plans that seem plausible—that are laid out on pretty charts and include carefully precise steps and almost always describe a fictional reality.

As I've said previously, the very act of planning is so seductive, so alluring, that planning itself becomes more important than the actual plan. And the plan becomes more important than reality. Never forget: the map is *not* the terrain.

When a team first sits down to map out a project, there is often electricity in the room—a sense of possibility, of new worlds to discover and new ideas with which to experiment. It really is one of the best feelings in the world.

Then comes that moment when inspiration turns to calculation, and some of that energy dissipates. People begin pondering: *How do we actually get from point A to point B? And once we've figured that out, how long is it going to take?*

Unfortunately, that calculation phase can be a garbage-in/garbage-out process. The people involved may be highly intelligent, and yet they typically won't *realize* that what they're feeding into their planning charts is a lot of wishful thinking.

When Mark had explained the situation at Medco, I replied, "You do have a problem." I waited a beat, then followed that with: "But I bet we can solve it."

Right before Christmas I flew to New Jersey to spend a day at the company, determining the scope of the issue. It was not trivial. There were reams of paper outlining requirements, compliance, all sorts of reports and phase-gates and quality assurance. Buried in there somewhere was what actually needed to be done, but no one actually had a plan for how to *do* it.

After meeting with key personnel for a while, I called up Brent Barton, a Scrum trainer I'd worked with on other projects. "Brent," I said, "I need you and whomever else you can wrangle by the beginning of January. We've got our work cut out for us."

Brent would later describe the Medco he saw when he walked in as a company in "deadlock." There were so many interests and people at loggerheads that nothing was getting done. That first day we met with about seven different groups of people, each of which owned a piece of the project, and none was really interested in trying something new. But, he says now, "We had the luxury of 'Oh, shit.' You can use pain and fear as your ally when you walk in as a consultant. When we ran into resistance, we just told them, 'Hey, you can do things the way you're doing them, stick with the status quo, and you'll deliver late, and that'll be fine.' And they said, 'That's not fine.'"

The first thing we did was call everyone into a conference room—all the key players, all the people who'd actually be doing the work. And Brent told everyone to print out all the documents they had describing what needed to be done with the project. No, e-mail wasn't okay; we wanted physical paper.

We were in a large room, maybe fifty feet on a side—windowless, as those kinds of rooms mysteriously always seem to be. In the middle was a table where we stacked all the documents that people walked in with a few hours later. The stack was at least two feet tall.

"How many of you have actually *read* all this?" I asked.

Silence.

"But look," I said to one of the managers, "you signed off on this. There's your signature. Didn't you actually read it?"

More awkward silence.

I didn't want to pick on him, but the fact is, in project after project, people cut and paste and throw in boilerplate, but no one actually reads all those thousands of pages. They can't. That's the point. They've set up a system that forces them to endorse a fantasy.

So Brent and I got out scissors and tape, glue sticks, and sticky notes. Turns out, you really *did* learn everything you need to know in kindergarten.

"Here's what we're going to do," Brent said. "We're going to go through these stacks of paper and cut out everything that is actually something that needs to be done to complete this project. Then we're going to stick them on the wall."

So over the next couple of hours that's what people did. At the end we had hundreds and hundreds of notes lining three walls. Still on the table was more than 50 percent of that two-foot tower. Duplication, boilerplate, templates. Complete and total waste.

Then I said to the teams, "Now we need to estimate how much work each one of these sticky notes will take." Not how long, but how much *work*.

I'll go into the best ways to do this later in this chapter, since humans are actually awful at estimating work. But I taught them a quick and dirty method that is the best of a whole bunch of bad ways of doing it, and they went at it.

It took them a while, but they did it. Up on the wall was everything they needed to do to complete the project, broken down into manageable tasks. And they'd estimated how much effort they thought each one would take. They actually were excited. An unreadable stack of paper had become understandable pieces of work. It's like that old saw, "How do you eat an elephant? One bite at a time."

One of the key things we did with each sticky note was write down not only what had to be created, but also how we'd know when it was done. This is how we incorporated all the FDA compliance requirements, quality assurance, and process reports they had to be mindful of. We simply said for this task to be done, it had to meet those goals. We baked that into the project at the work-item level, rather than waiting for everything to be done and then finding out that we weren't in compliance with some federal regulation or internal quality metric. This way everyone on the team, not only the compliance people, had to work to meet that level of quality first, before moving on to the next item. The amount of rework this removes from a project is incredible. I call this standard that must be met a "Definition of Done." Everyone knows when something is done or not; there are clear standards that any piece of work has to meet.

Staring at all those sticky notes on the wall, everyone had a feeling of accomplishment. They could now see what they had to do.

"Okay," Brent said. "What do we need to do first?"

About five people spoke up.

"And then?"

Another five people with different ideas this time.

"And then?"

What we wanted them to do was something that, at times, no one really wants to do: *prioritize the work*. Often people simply say everything is important. But what he was asking was, What will bring the most value to the project? Let's do those things first.

At the end we had six different rows of sticky notes on the walls, each a different color representing a different team. The lists stretched the length of three sides of the room. Now I knew we could at least begin.

Wedding Planning

It may sound simple when I put it that way, but let me illustrate the steps in the process by using an example that is smaller in scale: a wedding. A formal wedding is a project with a lot of things that have to be done by a particular date, and as you know, if you've gotten married—or will discover, if you do decide to wed—everything will go wrong and will take four times the effort you anticipated.

Of course, it can go the other way too: something that you think will take hours gets banged out in fifteen minutes. The ever-plaguing question is, Why are we so terrible at estimating how long something will take?

And, boy, are we bad. We'll get to that wedding in a moment, but first let me introduce you to a graph with one of the best names ever, the "Cone of Uncertainty" (see page 119).

The graph shows that beginning estimates of work can range from 400 percent beyond the time actually taken to 25 percent of the time taken. The low and high estimates differ by a factor of sixteen. As the project progresses and more and more gets settled, the estimates fall more and more into line with reality until there are no more estimates, only reality.

Think back to Medco. They spent months planning their

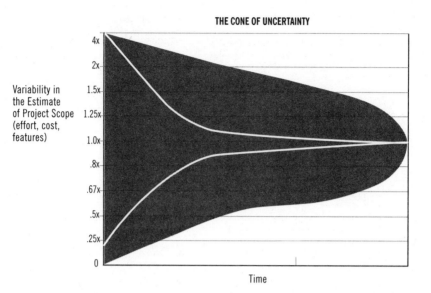

effort—what the product would look like, how long it would take. And even after all those months, the research shows that they were likely to be off by as much as a factor of four either way. Which is why, in my opinion, Waterfall-type planning is a really stupid way of doing things.

Okay, Sutherland, I can hear you saying, we're bad at estimating, but I've got to do *something*, right? I have to have some sort of plan. And you're right: you do. But the key is to refine the plan *throughout* the project rather than do it all up front. Plan in just enough detail to deliver the next increment of value, and estimate the remainder of the project in larger chunks. In Scrum, at the end of each iteration you have something of value that you can see, touch, and show to customers. You can ask them: "Is this what you want? Does this solve at least a piece of your problem? Are we going in the right direction?" And if the answer is no, change your plan.

So how do you do it?

Let's talk about that wedding. The first thing to do is create a list of all the things that make up a successful wedding. It might look something like this:

- Bride and Groom
- Flowers
- Invitations
- Church
- Reception Hall
- Food
- Officiant
- Dress
- Wedding Rings
- Music (DJ or Band)

Now, the next thing to do is to take all those elements and sort them by priority. And that's going to be different for different people. Every bride and every groom sees the world differently. But I asked my friend Alex the other day how he prioritized *his* list, and this is the order he came up with:

- Bride and Groom
- Officiant
- Wedding Rings
- Reception Hall
- Invitations
- Food
- Music
- Dress
- Flowers
- Church

The point of the exercise is to figure out the really important things and work on those first. For Alex, the food and music are more important than having the wedding in a church or the flowers. This is important data to have, because if you start bumping up against date or cost constraints, you know where to start cutting—at the bottom of the list. I'll get into more detail on this in chapter eight, but that's probably enough for now.

At Medco the list wrapped around three walls of a large conference room and was hundreds of items long with six different teams working on them. But the concept was entirely the same. Organize by value, whatever value that may be. It could be business value in the case of Medco, or it could be bride happiness value in the case of a wedding.

Size Does Matter, but Only Relatively

So you have your list of stuff that needs to be done, and you've prioritized that list. Now the job is to figure out just how much effort, time, and money the project will take. As I've already pointed out, we humans are absolutely terrible at this, but what we *are* good at, it turns out, is *relative* sizing—comparing one size to another. Picking out the difference between small, medium, and large T-shirts, for example.

My favorite example of relative sizing is "Dog Points." Several years ago a friend and one of the leading figures in Agile thinking, Mike Cohn, was, like me, struggling with how to make his projects come in on time and on budget, and how to estimate them. A dog lover, though his wife forbade him from getting a pooch, he started asking his teams what size of "dog" each piece of a project was. He'd list off a bunch of breeds. Like this:

- Labrador retriever
- Terrier
- Great Dane
- Poodle
- Dachshund
- German shepherd
- Irish setter
- Bulldog

And then he'd say, "Okay, this problem—is it a dachshund or a Great Dane? And if that one is a dachshund, this one must be about the size of a Labrador retriever, right?" And then the teams would go through all the features they had to develop and size them by dog. And then Mike would say, "Let's give each breed a number value; that'll be easier. Let's call a dachshund a one and a Great Dane a thirteen. That would make a Lab a five, say, and a bulldog a three."[1]

You could do the same thing with the wedding to-do list we just made. Finding a venue, well, that's going to take some research, some pricing information, visiting the places. It's kind of involved. Let's call it a German shepherd–size problem, a five. Bride and Groom? No problem: the two of us just have to show up. That's a dachshund, a one, just a phone call. Invitations, though, that is pretty involved. We have to make our list, get your mother's list, get my mother's list, pick out the stationery, have the invitations printed, hand address them. That's a big project. That's a Great Dane, a thirteen. Or maybe two Great Danes. And if something is that big, you should probably cut it down into manageable pieces. How about we make the gathering of the names one project and dealing with the printer another? Those are probably both the size of a bulldog, right? Call that a three. The addressing we'll call a German shepherd, a five. And so on.

So that's relative sizing, comparing tasks to one another. Now, we don't all use dogs, unfortunately, but you might have noticed a pattern there in the numbers I assigned: 1, 3, 5, 8, 13. Each number in the series is the sum of the two previous numbers. It's called the "Fibonacci sequence," and there's a reason we use it. It is everywhere.

Fibonacci Sequence: All Around Us

- The Fibonacci sequence is a pattern where the next number in the sequence is the sum of the previous two, e.g., 0, 1, 1, 2, 3, 5, 8, 13, 21, 34, 55 . . .

- Ubiquitous in natural systems, so humans have millennia of experience with it

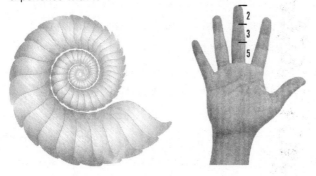

The sequence is how nature lays itself out, whether it be in the shell of a nautilus, the branches on a tree, the bumps on a pineapple, or the petals of a pinecone. It shows up in cauliflower and the curves of the human brain. It's the same whether you're looking at the curl of a fern leaf or the shape of a galaxy. It's one of those phenomena that, when you think about it, is pretty freaky.

There's a name for this phenomenon—it's called the "Golden

Mean" or the "Golden Ratio." We've built it into buildings and art. From the Parthenon in Athens to the Great Mosque of Kairouan in Tunisia. We've used it to decide the size and shape of pages in a book and the proportions of playing cards. Humans are just programmed to find the ratios attractive. For our purposes, all that's important to know is that our species deeply understands the ratios of the Fibonacci sequence. We know them in our bones.

The numbers in the Fibonacci sequence are far enough apart that we can easily tell the difference. It's easy for people to come down on one side or the other. If one person estimates something as a five, and another as an eight, we can intuitively see the difference. But the difference between a five and a six? That's pretty subtle, more than our brains can really register.

It's fairly well-known in medicine that for patients to report they perceive an improvement in a symptom, it has to have been a greater than 65-percent improvement. Our minds don't work in smooth increments. We're better at perceiving jumps from one state to another—and not smooth jumps but jagged ones.

What using the Fibonacci sequence to calculate task size permits is estimates that don't have to be 100 percent accurate. Nothing will be exactly a five or an eight or a thirteen, but using those numbers gives us a way to collect opinions on the size of a task where everyone is using roughly the same measuring stick, and in that way a consensus is formed.

Estimating as a group in this manner gives us a far more accurate estimate than we could come up with alone.

The Oracle of Delphi

So now we know we're good at comparing one thing to another. And we know the best ratio to utilize for the task. But how do we get there? A list of prioritized things to do is all well and good, but how do we figure out which story is a five and which is an eight; which is a goldie and which is a schnauzer? And even if one person has a pretty good idea, how do we make sure her estimates line up with everyone else's? What if she isn't taking some key factors into account?

Unsurprisingly, this is not a new problem. People have struggled for decades with exactly this. One issue is that different members of the team know different things, but another is sometimes called the "bandwagon" effect. You've been in meetings like that. That's when someone comes up with an idea, and everyone starts talking about it. And even if you disagreed with it initially, you go along because the group is going along. And everyone agrees on a path forward that seems like a really good idea at the time but turns out to be a complete failure. And when you probe people about the decision, it's almost always the case that each had some reservations, but they didn't voice them because they figured everyone else was excited. People assume that if everyone else is going along with something, their own reservation is silly or misinformed, and they don't want to look stupid in front of the group. Remember, this groupthink isn't an individual failure; this is a human failure.

In the literature this effect has been explained as an "informational cascade." As Sushil Bikhchandani, David Hirshleifer, and Ivo Welch, the authors of the paper "A Theory of Fads, Fashion, Custom, and Cultural Change as Informational Cascades" put it: "An informational cascade occurs when it is optimal for an individual, having observed the actions of those ahead of him, to follow the behavior of the preceding individual without regard to his own information."[2]

A great example the authors use is the submission of a paper to a journal. Let's say the first journal's editor rejects it. Then the writer submits the same article to a second journal. That journal's editor, learning of the first rejection, is more likely to reject it. And if there's a third journal, that editor, knowing of the two previous rejections, is even more likely to reject it. People assume other people are making sound judgments, *even if those judgments contradict their own.* This is bad. When you're making a judgment about when you'll likely deliver a multibillion-dollar project—or whether you'll get everything done on time for your wedding day—it's critical to apply your *own* judgment, and use other estimates to improve your own, not replace it.

The other well-known problem is what's called the "halo effect." This is when one characteristic of something influences how people perceive other, unrelated characteristics. This was first empirically studied in 1920 by Edward Lee Thorndike. In his classic paper "A Constant Error in Psychological Ratings," Thorndike asked military officers to rank their soldiers by various qualities—physical, intellectual, leadership, personality, and so on. He then looked at how one set of qualities affected the rating of another. He found that they correlated too closely. If someone's physique was rated highly, so were his leadership skills. And his intelligence. And his character. This research has been supported in follow-up studies over the years, confirming that, for example, if someone is good-looking, everyone assumes that they're also smart and trustworthy.[3]

But the halo effect extends to much more than mere physical beauty; it can crop up anywhere. Researchers point out, for example, that nongovernmental organizations (NGOs) are often treated as forces for good even if they aren't, that car companies will create one "halo" car to give a whole line a good impression, and that the Apple iPod gave all Apple's products a veneer of coolness.

As with the bandwagon effect, people who are focused on the "halo" don't look at actual data—rather, they gravitate toward something that has a positive sheen to it. Again, this isn't a failure of will; this is the nature of people. Fighting it head-on is silly—it's like fighting gravity.

But you can be clever about it. In the 1950s, the Rand Corporation was asked to answer some questions—the terrifying kind that got bandied about during the Cold War. Invoking in their terminology the Oracle of Delphi, the priestess who could predict the future, Norman Dalkey and Olaf Helmer published in 1963 a blandly titled paper, "An Experimental Application of the Delphi Method to the Use of Experts," with the helpful reference "Memorandum RM-727/1-Abridged." In the paper they declared their intention to pose questions without having one person's opinions affect those of another. So they gathered a group of experts: four economists, a physical-vulnerability specialist, a systems analyst, and an electrical engineer. And they proposed to

Apply expert opinion to the selection, from the viewpoint of a Soviet strategic planner, of an optimal U.S. industrial target system and to the estimation of the number of A-bombs required to reduce the munitions output by a prescribed amount.[4]

Or to put it more simply: the idea was to ask how many nukes the Russians needed to stop us from making our own nukes. This was back when a nuclear conflict was seen as not only possible, but winnable.

The thing is, Dalkey and Helmer didn't want their experts to

127

be influenced by one another. What if one was a department head at a big university and another a lowly faculty member at a small college? How to prevent one person's false assumptions from spoiling the opinions of others?

What the two researchers did was conduct a series of anonymous surveys. None of the experts knew who the others were; they were just to give their estimates. After each questionnaire, the research duo would take the answers—and data relied upon for those answers—and feed it back to the group with any identifying characteristics stripped away. Rinse and repeat.

So, in the first questionnaire the number of bombs needed to give a 50-percent confidence in the destruction of the US arms industry was estimated to fall in a range from 50 at the low end to 5,000 at the high end. When Dalkey and Helmer analyzed the answers, it seemed that there were some commonalities in thinking—the vulnerability of various targets, the recoverability of various industries, initial stockpiles, and so on. They then asked the experts if that breakdown was correct, and what other information they used in coming up with their answers.

And they got back everything from how sturdy the factories were to the difference between physical and economic vulnerability to the lead time in manufacturing various components.

Dalkey and Helmer then took that data, gave it to all the experts, and said, okay, now how many bombs? Now the range was between 89 and 800. Then they did it again. And again. The results kept getting narrower. Eventually the range was down to between 167 and 360 nuclear weapons needed.

Being able to winnow an impossibly wide range of estimates— from 10,000 percent to about 200 percent—is an incredibly powerful capability for policy makers. It allows them to get a general expert consensus without worries of bias. This tool is so powerful that it is still used today by Rand. Just one recent example was a 2011 Delphi exercise looking at the conflict in Afghanistan and estimating the United States's chances of success. The outlook, if you're interested, was not great.

Planning Poker

So the advantage of Delphi is that it takes a broad array of opinions, attempts to remove as much bias as possible, and with informed, yet anonymous, statements narrows down opinions into a generally accepted estimate. The bad part, for our purposes, is that it takes a long time. When I sat down with the teams at Medco, I didn't spend any time with anonymous surveys. I wanted all those hundreds of items estimated within *hours*, not days, and certainly not weeks.

Fortunately, there *is* a way of gathering estimates that is fairly quick and accurate. It's called "Planning Poker."

The idea is simple. Each person has a deck of cards with those oh-so-interesting Fibonacci numbers on them—1, 3, 5, 8, 13, and so on. Each item that needs to be estimated is brought to the table. Then everyone pulls the card they think represents the right amount of effort and puts it facedown on the table. At the same time everyone flips the cards over. If everyone is within two cards of each other (say a five, two eights, and a thirteen), the team just adds them all up and takes the average (in that case 6.6) and moves on to the next item. Remember, we're talking *estimates*, not iron-bound schedules. And estimates on small pieces of the project.

If people are more than *three* cards apart, then the high and the low cards talk about why they think what they do. Then everyone does another round of Planning Poker. Otherwise they just average the estimates, which will approximate the numbers that the statisticians at the Rand Corporation came up with.

Here's an example: Let's say you're painting the interior of a house, and you need to estimate how long it will take to paint the living room, the kitchen, and two bedrooms. And you're doing this with a team that you've painted rooms with before. So first the two bedrooms: everyone estimates those at a three. No real disagreement; you've all done this before and see bedrooms as fairly straightforward. Then the team estimates the living room. It's a pretty big room but fairly simple. People's estimates run from five to thirteen, eventually averaging six. Again, no need for discussion. Then comes the kitchen, and there's a three, an eight, a thirteen, and a five on the table. The person with the three argues that the room is pretty small, involving even less wall space than the bedrooms. The person with the thirteen counters that the real time sink is all the taping of cabinets and counters they'll have to do, and that painting all those small areas will have to be done with a brush, not with a roller. The team quickly lays down new cards. Now the three has become an eight, and everyone else stays the same. Close enough, they add them all up, average, and move on to the next task.

This incredibly simple method is a way to avoid any kind of anchoring behavior, such as the bandwagon or halo effects, and it allows the whole team to share knowledge on a particular task. It's crucial, though, that you have the team who's actually doing the work do the estimating, not some expert "ideal" estimators.

I learned this the hard way when I was working with an e-commerce company in Pennsylvania, GSI Commerce. They've since been bought up by eBay. What GSI does is design the online stores for such companies as Levi's, Toys "R" Us, Major League Baseball, and Zales Diamonds. These are not small projects. And GSI is pretty good at it.

But GSI had the idea, which seemed like a good idea at the time, that instead of having each individual team do the estimates, they'd assign the task to the best estimators in the company—the smartest guys in the room who really understood the projects and the technology and knew what needed to be done. So they took some projects and estimated them. This one should take this much time, the next one that much, and so on. The plan was to deliver estimates for eighty multimillion-dollar projects to both their clients and the teams that would actually do the work. This seems reasonable, right?

Well, it turns out to be such a *wrong* way of going about things that they stopped the experiment halfway through, after forty projects were done. I was reminded of those drug studies that are halted because it turns out the drugs are killing the patients instead of curing them. The estimates were so far off, they were useless.

Nothing was delivered on time. Customers were unhappy. The teams were demoralized. It was a complete disaster. The managers went back to having the teams that would be doing the work also do the estimation. Lo and behold, the estimates once again started lining up with reality.

What I took away from that was that only the people doing the work know how long and how much effort it will take. Maybe their team is really good at one kind of thing but terrible at another. Maybe they have one expert who can be helpful in a particular area, but no one on the team knows about a different area. Teams, as I've discussed before, are individual and unique. Each has its own pace and rhythm. Forcing them into cookie-cutter processes is a recipe for disaster.

There Are No Tasks; There Are Only Stories

When you list things that need to be done, it's tempting just to put together a list as I did earlier about Alex's wedding: church, flowers, officiant, food, etc. The problem is, if you give any of those items to a separate team that isn't intimately invested in the results of the decisions between white roses and daisies, you might not get the results you're looking for.

How many times at work have you been given a job where you don't understand the reason you're doing it? Someone asks you to determine how much sales changed from month to month in Region A, looking at stores with more than 600 square feet. You do it, but you don't know *why* it needs to be done. And because of that, you might provide the wrong kind of data, you might misinterpret the question, or you might just get resentful at being given a bunch of what seems like busywork. Or if you're the manager, you might be astounded that your people don't understand immediately that you're looking at closing down small stores and opening up big ones.

The problem is that you're not getting, or giving, enough information to actually do the job right. People think in narratives, in stories. That's how we understand the world. We have an intimate grasp of characters, desires, and motivations. Where we get into trouble is when we try to abstract out of the main through-line discrete parts and deal with them out of context.

So the first thing you want to think about when you're considering a task is character or role—for example, a customer, a bride, a reader, an employee. *Who* is this task being done for? Whose lens on the world is the one we need to gaze through when we're building this thing, making that decision, or delivering this piece?

Then you need to think of the *what*—what we want done in the first place. This is usually where we start and stop. But it's only the middle of the process we should be following.

Finally, you need to think of motivation. *Why* does this character want this thing? How is it going to serve and delight this particular customer? And, in a way, this is the key part. Motivation colors everything.

My favorite example of this comes from an Internet meme from a few years back. It's simply a picture of Captain Jean-Luc Picard of the USS *Enterprise*, under which the text reads: "As a starship captain, I'd like the log function to automatically use today's stardate. . . ." It makes sense when you think about it. Haven't you wondered why in the far future a starship captain would have to state the date when he makes a log entry? "Captain's Log. Stardate 4671.7. The planet Mars is lovely from orbit. . . ." *We* don't have to do that now when we make a blog entry. Why does he?

But the key question not answered in that picture is *why*. Why does he want that functionality? What purpose will it serve? Is it just to keep entries in date order? Or is it more serious? Do those logs have to be unalterable to serve some sort of audit functionality by Starfleet crime-scene investigators? Those are two very different implementations. One casual, one robust. The team needs to figure out what he really wants to do, at which point they might think of a wholly different way to do it, with more relevant information that the captain may not have even thought of but that would be really useful.

Often, needs will change with different characters. Imagine, for example, a story with the back two-thirds: ". . . I want a car so that I can drive to work." Now, if you start that sentence with "As a suburban commuter . . ." versus "As a farmer in the South Dakota Badlands . . . ," you are going to end up with a very different interpretation of what the ideal vehicle is.

So before you prioritize what needs to be done for your business, you need to define the character, the user, the customer—the person who's going to use what you're going to do. You need to know their likes, dislikes, passions, enthusiasms, frustrations, and joys. And then you need to understand their motivations. How do those character types feed what they want? Why do they need a car? What are they going to do with that captain's log?

This will also influence how you'll estimate things. Oh, they want a simple calendar function; that's easy. An unalterable time stamp for legal purposes—that's a bit trickier.

Write Short Stories

When you're writing your stories, though, you want to make sure that they're small enough that you can actually estimate them. Imagine the story about Amazon.com: *As a customer, I want the world's biggest online bookseller so that I can buy any book I want at any time I want.* Now, that certainly encapsulates Amazon, but it's really too big to actually do anything with. You need to break it down. Really down.

You might write stories like these for an online bookstore:

> "As a customer, I want to be able to browse books by genre, so that I can find the type of books I like."

> "As a customer, I want to put a book into a shopping cart, so that I can buy it."

> "As a product manager, I want to be able to track a customer's purchases, so that I can market specific books to her based on past purchases."

Those stories are ones that a team can wrap its head around. A discussion can actually ensue about how to implement them. They're specific enough to be actionable but don't prescribe *how* they're going to be done. Remember, the team decides how the work will be accomplished, but *what* will be accomplished is decided by business value. The whole collection of stories that might make up that idea of an online bookstore is often referred to as an "Epic"—a story too big to do by itself but that includes a number of smaller stories that add up to a single idea.

Tim Stoll is one of those guys whose career spans what might be called a "broad spectrum of events," with a focus on getting teams to get things done fast. He was a Special Forces medic who saw service in Iraq and Afghanistan, a CIA contractor, and a police officer whose job it was to go after violent felons, and he's now a Scrum coach. He's *always* been a Scrum coach, he says, even when he was leading Special Forces missions.

"In Special Operations," he says, "we don't call them stories. We call them Courses of Action. But they're the same thing."

Here's one of the few stories Tim can tell publicly about a Special Forces mission—a medical mission to Laos. "We had two Epics. The first was a medical course of instruction—training local forces on combat medicine. The second epic was a de-mining operation dealing with unexploded ordnance."

As the medic, Tim was in charge of that first Epic. He says that before the mission he sat down and figured out what he needed to accomplish and how he should order the substories. And, he says, he started with ideas that fall very easily into the Scrum framework.

"As a Special Forces medic, I must teach basic physiology to my students, so they can understand the human body."

Tim says that he knew he had to start there as he began writing his stories. His students had to understand where the bones were to do any sort of first aid. "First, I'd teach long bones, then short bones, then wrists, ankles, tendons, ligaments." Only after the basic stories were covered could he get into setting those bones, clearing airways, and stopping bleeding.

After writing those stories he could see what he needed to support his teaching objectives. He needed a skeleton. He needed handouts in English and Laotian. And then he broke everything into iterations or Sprints. "Two days flying to Laos. One week of setup. Then two six-week iterations on instruction. We had to bring our students up from basic to EMT intermediate. And we did it."

Be Ready and Be Done

When you're writing stories or making a list of work to be done, it's important to ask two questions: Is the story ready? And how will you know when it's done?

Let's take Tim's story as an example:

As a Special Forces medic, I must teach basic physiology to my students, so they can understand the human body.

There is a mnemonic I always use to tell whether a story is ready. It was created by Bill Wake, who's a deep thinker on software design. Bill says that for any story to be ready it needs to meet the INVEST criteria:

Independent. The story must be actionable and "completable" on its own. It shouldn't be inherently dependent on another story.

Negotiable. Until it's actually being done, it needs to be able to be rewritten. Allowance for change is built in.

Valuable. It actually delivers value to a customer or user or stakeholder.

Estimable. You have to be able to size it.

Small. The story needs to be small enough to be able to estimate and plan for easily. If it is too big, rewrite it or break it down into smaller stories.

Testable. The story must have a test it is supposed to pass in order to be complete. Write the test before you do the story.

So Tim's story is independent; he can accomplish his mission without having to consider, say, the helicopter fuel it will take the students to get to the site. His story is negotiable: teaching physiology is the story he thinks he needs to do, but if he gets there and finds out that the students already have this knowledge, or part of this knowledge, he can change his teaching approach. It's valuable: the students will learn practical and applicable knowledge of the human body. It's small: it's basic anatomy, not how to do surgery given the amount of anatomy he will be teaching. And it's testable: he knows the information he wants to impart, and he can give his students a test to see if they've actually learned the information.

For each story pursued there should be both a "definition of Ready" (as in "Does it meet the INVEST criteria?") and finally "a definition of Done" (as in "What conditions need to be met, what tests need to be passed, to call it a wrap?"). We find in real projects that if stories are really Ready, the team will double the speed of implementation. And if the stories are really Done at the end of a Sprint, teams can double speed again. This is one of the tricks needed to get twice as much work done in half the time.

Sprint Planning

In Scrum this kind of planning happens with each and every Sprint at what is called the "Sprint Planning" meeting. Everyone gets together and looks at the list of stories that have to be done and says, "Okay, what can we accomplish at *this* Sprint? Are these stories ready? Can they be done by the end of this iteration? Can we then demo them to the customer and show real value?" The key to answering those questions lies in just how fast the team is going.

Know Your Velocity

We can finally start answering the question as to when things will be done, because we now know how to measure what the team is actually doing. We have all these stories—these things that need to be done. And we've estimated them—this one is an eight, this one a three, and so on. And then we start on our first Sprint. Let's say it's a week long. At the end of the week we count up all the stories we've completed, total the points they were estimated at, and that number tells us how fast the team is going, their velocity. And once you have a velocity, you can look at how many stories you have left and how many points they represent, and then you know when you'll be done.

Also once you have your velocity, you can figure out the most important thing in Scrum: what is keeping you from going *faster*? What is keeping you from *accelerating*? In the last chapter I talked about waste, about the things that will slow you down. This is how you see if you really *are* getting rid of waste.

Let's go back to Medco, where we started this chapter. After we'd estimated all the work, I sat down with the senior management responsible for the project. There were several VPs who were general managers of business units and a Senior VP.

We sat down at the conference table, and that Senior Vice President had only one question. "Will you meet the original date?" he asked, slapping his hand on the table.

"I don't know," I said. "But we'll beat the revised date your people came up with, or you can get your money back."

"That's not good enough! Will you meet the original date?"

"I can't tell you that *today*. We have to get the teams moving to see how fast they are. I'll tell you what: in six weeks I'll give you our delivery date, and it isn't going to be one you'll like. But,"

I said quickly before he could interrupt, "I'll give you a list of the things that are getting in your teams' way, that are stopping them from meeting that July date you promised Wall Street. A list of impediments. And your job will be to remove them as fast as possible."

He laughed. "Impediments! No problem, Jeff. I used to work at Toyota."

I laughed and said, "This looks like a good project already."

I knew that he'd embraced Taiichi Ohno's taxonomy of waste and understood how things worked—that getting rid of waste was the key to accelerating teams.

And so after three Sprints of measuring velocity, the teams had accelerated from 20 to 60 points per sprint and I knew when the teams would likely deliver. Given the velocity of the teams, and we were now at the beginning of March, it would take them another nineteen two-week Sprints—December 1.

Management wasn't happy. Not good enough. It was July 1 or nothing. Everything was riding on it.

Then I handed them a memo with a list of twelve impediments on it. They ranged from not empowering people to make decisions to onerous technical requirements, from people not showing up for meetings to simple things such as not having everybody on a team work in the same room. There were process, personality, and procedure problems—the type of things that are endemic to any corporation.

These kinds of impediments can seem insurmountable. How often have you looked around at your own workplace and thought, *We do it this way, we've always done it this way, and everyone knows it's dumb.* But for some reason people see corporate-cultural change as impossible. I used to agree with them, especially when it came to big companies with an ossified culture and policies.

Medco proved me wrong, and I'll never go back to my old way of thinking. That Senior Vice President from Toyota sent out our memo to his entire staff on a Monday. Each impediment had a manager's name next to it. And each one of the impediments was gone by Thursday. Maybe to be motivated to change, people sometimes need a gun to their head, but it showed what can be done if the will is there (or if you have a guy from Toyota in charge). Nothing is written in stone. Question everything.

By the end of the next Sprint, the teams' velocity had gone up 50 percent. The new date for delivery was September 1. Still three months late even though they had accelerated from 20 points to 90 points per Sprint, over 400 percent!

And still not good enough.

So Brent and I gathered everyone together, from engineering to marketing to business analysts to compliance folks to management. And they were afraid. They were afraid for their jobs and careers if they couldn't pull this off. So, I asked them three questions:

1. Is there anything we can do differently to speed things up?

   "Well," said the head of engineering, "during the middle of the last Sprint the IT security guys shut off a port to the Internet, so our teams in India and Brazil couldn't get anything done."

   "Well, we should fix that, shouldn't we?" I said in disbelief. The head of engineering looked at the head of IT, who was sitting farther down the table. They thought that might knock another month off the time it would take to deliver the product. Two months to go.

2. Can we offload some Backlog items? Is there stuff we can get other teams to do?

No one had any good ideas.

3. Can we *not do* some things? Can we reduce the scope of the project by any amount?

Originally, they told me no way, that they'd already cut to the bone on requirements. Okay, I said, but let's just spend the afternoon whittling away at it. Every single task has to fight for its life.

It took a few hours, but we got another month off delivery.

That's when I said, okay, we're still a month off the date. If we can't figure out something else, we're going to need to tell management we can't do it.

"No," everyone replied, "we'll all get fired. Let's take a look at those three questions again." I proposed we meet with the management team. It was not just our problem. It was their problem as well, and they could help.

It was a short meeting. Management looked at the situation and said, "Well, we have to deliver on July 1. Maybe we could just roll it out to one factory first? One center? Or only a couple? Would that work?" There was some hemming and hawing and rearranging of a few things. But they eventually figured out that they could reduce the features needed and meet the July 2007 date the president had promised Wall Street.

At the end of that meeting the Senior Vice President simply said, "Let's declare victory. Call us if you run into any problems."

It was amazing to watch the stock price of Medco that summer. When we started building the infrastructure, the stock started going up, and when we delivered, it continued to rise. How much? Well, many billions of dollars' worth, from a price of 25 to over 50 within the year. Wall Street had decided the company would continue to grow, would attract new customers, and would maintain its leadership in the field. In retrospect, I should have asked for a percentage-of-market-cap increase rather than a simple fee.

A few years later Medco used Scrum to build what they called "Medco 2.0." They restructured every part of the company, from the steel out. New factories, new robots, new processes, more automation. Mark Landy, who by then was the Chief Technical Officer of the company, says that without the Therapeutic Resource Center experience they couldn't have done it. "They wouldn't have allowed us to do it enterprise wide. But we had the confidence of the entire organization: Development, Operations, Finance, Clinical. We were able to make a new culture." And that, he says, is the most important part of Scrum: it changes the culture people work in, which can be scary for some. Indeed, the company had to get rid of employees who couldn't make the switch, he says—not because they were incompetent, but because they were hoarding information and knowledge for their own benefit, to ensure their own indispensability rather than helping the team and the company. Changing that culture, though, is what allows true excellence to emerge.

THE TAKEAWAY

The Map Is Not the Terrain. Don't fall in love with your plan. It's almost certainly wrong.

Only Plan What You Need To. Don't try to project everything out years in advance. Just plan enough to keep your teams busy.

What Kind of Dog Is It? Don't estimate in absolute terms like hours—it's been proven that humans are terrible at that. Size things relatively, by what breed of dog the problem is, or T-shirt size (S, M, L, XL, XXL), or, more commonly, the Fibonacci sequence.

Ask the Oracle. Use a blind technique, like the Delphi method, to avoid anchoring biases such as the halo effect or bandwagon effect or just plain stupid groupthink.

Plan with Poker. Use Planning Poker to quickly estimate work that needs to be done.

Work Is a Story. Think first about who'll be getting value from something, then about what it is, and then why they need it. Humans think in narratives, so give them one. As an *X*, I want *Y*, so that *Z*.

Know Your Velocity. Every team should know exactly how much work they can get done in each Sprint. And they should know how much they can improve that velocity by working smarter and removing barriers that are slowing them down.

Velocity × Time = Delivery. Once you know how fast you're going, you'll know how soon you'll get there.

Set Audacious Goals. With Scrum it is not that hard to double production or cut delivery time in half. If you do it in the *right way,* your revenue and stock price should double as well.

CHAPTER SEVEN

Happiness

People want to be happy. Not happy in a complacent, sheeplike way, but in a way that is more active. Thomas Jefferson, among many others, extolled the kind of happiness that comes from a pursuit. Pursuits do seem to be what make us happy. Scrum done in the *right way* will make workers, customers, managers, and stockholders happy (usually in that order).

Real happiness doesn't come easy. I met a mountain climber once who sold me a photo of the top of the Himalayas as the sun was setting. He took it shortly after he reached the peak of Mount Everest solo too late in the day. It seemed impossible to get back to base camp before dark. If he didn't, he was certain to freeze to death. The poignancy of the photo reflected his feelings as he wrote what he thought might be his last note, that he was happy to have achieved the peak despite the fact that whoever may read the note might find him dead.

If you speak to mountain climbers about an expedition, they won't spend much time talking about the experience of summiting a peak. Instead, they'll talk about the frigid temperatures, the painful blisters, the bad food, the crappy conditions, and the balky equipment. And they'll tell you that, after the elation of reaching the summit, there's usually a letdown (unless the near-death experience continues). They've done it. Their struggle has achieved something. But if you ask them when they were happiest, they'll tell you it was in those moments of trial—of pushing their bodies, minds, and spirits to the limit. *That's* when they were the happiest, when they experienced true joy. And that's what they want to experience again. On the face of it, no sane person would voluntarily put herself through that kind of thing *twice*. Yet climbers seem unable to stop themselves, challenging peak after peak, seeking joy in pursuit of the next summit.

What's fascinating is that most cultures are not set up to reward and encourage that specific type of happiness. Professor Tal Ben-Shahar taught the most popular course at Harvard University, "Positive Psychology." In his book *Happier,* Ben-Shahar writes: "We are not rewarded for enjoying the journey itself but for the successful *completion* of a journey. Society rewards results, not processes; arrivals, not journeys."

But our day-to-day life is mostly made up of journeys. We don't summit peaks every day, or make the big score, or get a big bonus. Most of our days are taken up with striving *toward* our goals, whatever they may be. In a company, the goal may be to deliver that next great product, or make people's lives a little better with it, or solve some problem that vexes the world. But if we get rewarded only for results, not processes, we're going to be pretty miserable.

When I first left academia for the business world in the early 1980s, I was put in charge of dozens of computer programmers who were miserable. Their projects were always late and over budget— and that's when the projects worked at all. Their mood became so negative that the energy in the room brought everyone down. The process they used was so broken, it was impossible to succeed. I've spent the last thirty years addressing that type of problem.

The importance of happiness really hit me when I was setting up my first Scrum team. I realized that I had to address the team's emotional state as well as its mental state. For a West Point–trained fighter pilot, this was something of an adjustment. I was used to things being cut-and-dried. Being clinical and scientific, it took me some time to figure out that to empower people, to change their lives for the better, I had to change myself. Over the course of that first Scrum effort I realized that true greatness is deeply rooted in joy. And that to be joyful is to take the first step toward success.

If all that sounds a little New Agey, or as if I'm about to tell you to sit around a campfire and sing "Kumbayah," you should know that in my early days of advising start-ups, the venture capitalists I worked with thought I was a flower child from San Francisco. Empowering people would never work in their worldview. Of course, these days I'm a senior consultant to venture firms and I'm often treated like an oracle. When people have a hard problem, they ask the oracle for the solution. They don't necessarily expect the answer to make sense. They just try it, and, to their surprise, it almost always works.

That's because happiness is crucial to your business and is actually a better forward predictor of revenue than most of the metrics your CFO provides. In this chapter I'm going to lay out just how important happiness is to your bottom line, and how to capture, measure, and apply it. This is happiness with rigor.

I may have become a better person through developing Scrum, which makes my family and me happier. But as a businessman and a scientist, I like hard data.

Happiness Is Success

The research is startlingly clear. Happy people simply do better—at home, at work, in life. They make more money, they have better jobs, they graduate from college, and they live longer. It's quite remarkable. Almost universally they're just better at what they do.

Happy people sell more stuff, make more money, cost less, are less likely to leave their jobs, are healthier, and live longer. Or as a 2005 paper that did a meta-analysis of some 225 papers with over 275,000 participants put it:

> Happiness leads to success in nearly every domain of our lives, including marriage, health, friendship, community involvement, creativity, and, in particular, our jobs, careers, and businesses.[1]

The meta-analysts showed that people who felt happy were more likely to secure job interviews, be evaluated more positively by supervisors, show superior performance and productivity, and be better managers.

Here's the really interesting part, though. It intuitively makes sense that happy people do better—it's *because* of their success that they're happy, right? Wrong. From that same meta-analysis: "Study after study shows that happiness *precedes* important outcomes and indicators of thriving."

That's right. People aren't happy because they're successful; they're successful because they're happy. Happiness is a *predictive* measure. And performance improves even if people are only a little bit happier. You don't have to change someone's life dramatically to make them happier, at least temporarily. Even just a little bit of happiness leads to markedly better outcomes. People don't have to be deliriously, wedding-day happy, just a little bit happier than they were. Of course, making them even happier has an even greater effect. But the message I want you to take away from this is simple: *even small gestures can have great impact.* What Scrum is focused on is taking those small things and systematically building them up into a scaffolding for success. Just one thing at a time, and you can actually change the world.

I'm going to give you a tool kit to measure your happiness and the happiness of your team, company, and family, as well as any organization you happen to be involved with. That is what Scrum does. Forget trust-building exercises, and instead build trust every single day. And I want you to measure it. It's not enough to *think* people are happy. I want you to be a scientist about it: quantify it and equate it with performance. If something doesn't match up, there's a problem. It's great to go to the pub with your team and bond. But it doesn't do the company a lot of good if that bonding doesn't actually translate into better performance. There are a lot of people I hang with just for fun. With my team I want that social aspect to move directly into performance. And it does.

Quantifying Happiness

How do we make ourselves, our employees, and our fellow team members happy? How do we channel that happiness into greater productivity and revenue?

To answer those questions, I need to take you back to Toyota and Taiichi Ohno's crusade to eliminate waste. That goal led him to the idea of "continuous improvement." It isn't enough to reach a certain level of productivity and stay there; the idea is to constantly examine your processes so as to improve them constantly and forever. Perfection can never be reached, of course, but every increment in that direction counts.

Just as work needs to be broken down into manageable chunks and time needs to be broken down into manageable pieces, improvement needs to be sliced to a step at a time. In Japanese the word used is *kaizen*, or "improvement." What is the little improvement that can be done right away that will make things better?

In Scrum this is captured at the end of each Sprint in what I call the "Sprint Retrospective." After the team has shown what they've accomplished during the last Sprint—that thing that is "Done" and can potentially be shipped to customers for feedback— they sit down and think about what went right, what could have gone better, and what can be made better in the next Sprint. What is the improvement in the process that they, as a team, can implement right away?

To be effective, this meeting requires a certain amount of emotional maturity and an atmosphere of trust. The key thing to remember is that you're not seeking someone to blame; you're looking at the process. Why did that happen that way? Why did we miss that? What could make us faster? It is crucial that people *as a team* take responsibility for their process and outcomes, and seek solutions *as a team*. At the same time, people have to have the fortitude to bring up the issues that are really bothering them in a way that is solution oriented rather than accusatory. And the rest of the team has to have the maturity to hear the feedback, take it in, and look for a solution rather than get defensive.

The Retrospective meeting is the "Check" part of Deming's Plan-Do-Check-Act cycle. The key is getting to that "Act" step, that *kaizen,* which will actually change the process and make it better the next time. It's not good enough merely to share how you feel; you need to be able to act.

The best way I've found to capture all this is with what I call the "Happiness Metric." It's a simple but very effective way of getting at what the *kaizen* should be, but also which *kaizen* will make people the happiest. And I've used it with pretty remarkable results.

Here's how it works. At the end of each Sprint each person on the team answers just a few questions:

1. On a scale from 1 to 5, how do you feel about your role in the company?
2. On the same scale, how do you feel about the company as a whole?
3. Why do you feel that way?
4. What one thing would make you happier in the next Sprint?

That's it. It can be done in just a few minutes. Every person on the team takes a turn, and it sparks really insightful conversations. Together the team usually comes up with a *kaizen* quite quickly. The method exposes what is most important to each team member, and what they think is most important for the company.

And here's the crucial piece. The team takes that one top improvement and makes it the most important thing to do in the next Sprint—*with acceptance tests*. How can you prove you've made that improvement? You need to define what success is in a concrete, actionable way, so that in the next Sprint Retrospective it's really easy to see if you achieved the *kaizen*.

A couple of years ago I decided to expand my company, Scrum, Inc., into a full-service Scrum consultancy. We tracked our velocity and found we were finishing about forty points of stories every one-week Sprint. When I implemented the Happiness Metric, the first thing that emerged was that our user stories weren't good enough. They weren't ready enough, they didn't have a definition of Done, and they were too vague. I worked on it, and we started to get better stories. During the next Sprint, the user stories still weren't good enough. Our Happiness numbers reflected that. In the third Sprint, another issue emerged. We addressed it. And so it went. In just a few weeks our velocity accelerated from forty points per sprint to 120. We tripled productivity simply by asking what would make people happier. As a result, our customers were happier, and our revenue dramatically shot up. All I had to do was start asking the team, "What would make you happier?" and then deliver on it.

We graphed this data over time and saw some extraordinarily interesting things. As a CEO, I'm focused on what's going to happen in the future to our revenue, growth, and productivity. Unlike with financial metrics, I've found the Happiness Metric to be *predictive.* Financials look at what happened in the past, but when you ask people how happy they are, they actually project into the future. And when they think about how happy they are with the company, they start projecting out how they think the company is doing. As a result, you'll get indications *before* a problem arises that one is coming. And if you pay close enough attention to what your team is telling you, you can take action and fix the issue before it becomes a problem. In the graph on page 153, for instance, a drop in happiness precedes a drop in velocity or productivity by weeks. If you were only looking at productivity, you wouldn't know that there was a problem until it dropped off a cliff. But if you see a team-wide drop in happiness, even as productivity is increasing, you know you have an issue that you need to address, and soon.

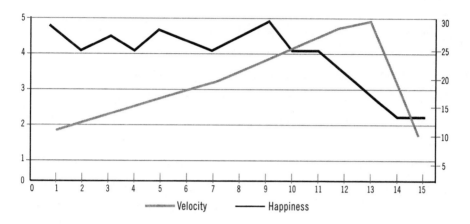

Make Everything Visible

What are the things that *actually* make people happy? They're the same things that make great teams: autonomy, mastery, and purpose. Or to say it more expansively, it's the ability to control your own destiny, it's the feeling that you're getting better at something, and it's knowing that you're serving something bigger than yourself. But there are also some easy, concrete steps management can take to get the culture of the company to encourage those qualities.

One element of Scrum that's often a prelude to achieving autonomy, mastery, and purpose is transparency. The idea is that there should be no secret cabal, no hidden agendas, nothing behind the curtain. Far too often in a company it isn't really clear what everyone is working on, or how each person's daily activity advances the goals of the company.

When I was starting Scrum, I spent a lot of time thinking about the laws a good friend of mine was influential in introducing into the Colorado legislature—"Sunshine" laws. They require that all public meetings be open, all records be available to the public, and that there be nothing taking place behind closed doors—nothing hidden. That's why in Scrum anyone can go to any meeting. Any stakeholder can observe a Daily Stand-up or attend a Review.

What I wanted to do was to make everything visible. And this can be scary to some people. PatientKeeper is a company that develops handheld applications for hospitals and doctors. When I was hired into the company, I immediately made all of engineering a Scrum shop. I told the developers that everyone would know everything. They were so used to seeing measurements getting used to beat them up that the new level of transparency made them afraid they'd only be abused more.

"Trust me," I said. "This won't be used to hurt you. Or punish you. It will only be used to make things better."

As I've said before, I'm not very interested in individual performance; I'm only interested in team performance. I can double a team's productivity in a month, but an individual? That could take a year. And a whole bunch of individuals? A whole division? A whole company? That could take forever. So I use transparency to focus on improving the team. I find that the team itself usually can address individual performance issues. They actually know what people are doing, who is helping, who is hurting, who makes the team great, and who makes it painful.

So in Scrum, everything is visible. In my companies, every salary, every financial, every expenditure is available to everyone. I've never understood why anyone would want to keep this stuff secret except to further their own individual agenda, or to keep people infantilized. I want the administrative assistant to be able to read the profit-and-loss statement and to understand *precisely* how what he does contributes to that. I want everyone in the company to be aligned with a unified purpose. Atomizing people into informational silos simply slows everyone down. Plus, it breeds suspicion and distrust. It divides a company into the big boys who know stuff and the peons who merely execute segments of some mysterious agenda they aren't capable of understanding. Bullshit. If you can't trust the people you're hiring to be on board with what you're doing, you're hiring the wrong people, and you've set up a system that has failure built in.

The most dramatic visual representation of this idea, and one you'll see in every Scrum team room across the planet, is the Scrum board.

PROJECT/ TEAM: AWESOME SCRUM TEAM				
BACKLOG	TO DO	IN PROGRESS	IN REVIEW/Q&A	DONE!

Now, there is software out there that can measure all sorts of things, give you all sorts of metrics and analysis, but a Scrum board is just a bunch of sticky notes on a whiteboard. There are three task-status levels: To Do, Doing, and Done. When someone signs out a story, everyone knows who's working on it. And everyone knows when it's done. And because the board has sticky notes that represent everything that needs to be done in a single Sprint, everyone knows how the Sprint is going. Anyone can walk into the room, glance at the board, and know exactly how the team is doing.

Because the team knows what has been done and what still needs to be done, they can regulate themselves. They know what they have to do, they can see if a colleague is in trouble, if a story has been in the Doing column too long. The team can self-organize to defeat problems that become obvious once everything is transparent.

At PatientKeeper the transparency that those developers were initially wary of paid off. Because all the work was transparent, we were able to coordinate assignments across multiple teams. Everyone knew exactly what everyone else was working on all the time. They could support one another if someone ran up against a roadblock. One developer might have already come up with a solution to a problem another developer faced, even if they weren't on the same team! Productivity at PatientKeeper increased more than four times. We released a production version of an enterprise software product forty-five times a year. This isn't Angry Birds updating; this is stuff deployed at major hospitals that people's lives depend on. But because we were transparent with everything, we could get the product into the market faster than anyone in the world. That's what Sunshine can do.

After I left PatientKeeper, a new management team decided Scrum wasn't the best way to run things anymore. The result? Product releases dropped from forty-five a year to two, revenue dropped from fifty million dollars a year to twenty-five, and attrition, which had been less than 10 percent, shot up to over 30 percent. They went from a great company back to mediocre performance by returning to traditional corporate behavior.

Delivering Happiness

One company that views happiness as core to their culture is Zappos. The wildly successful website convinced people to do something a lot of folks thought couldn't be done: buy shoes over the Internet. CEO Tony Hsieh wrote a book about it, *Delivering Happiness*. Tony writes about the unique culture at Zappos, which is based on creating "Wow!" moments for customers. It turns out that to make customers happy, you want happy people on the other end of the phone.

In talking to executives at Zappos, one of the words you hear a lot is *connection*. Their research shows that the more connected people are to other people at work, the happier they are—and, apparently, the more productive and innovative as well. So the company execs have set out deliberately to create these connections—not only on one team, or in one department, but across the whole company. And not just between people at one level, but between different levels, everyone from VPs to Accounts Receivable clerks.

They do this through means both simple and complex. For example, they physically encourage chance encounters. Their building has many exits, but they're all closed, save one, forcing people to go in and out through one door. The idea is that by having people bump into one another, they'll more likely create, and nurture, those connections.

Another example relates to the way people are brought into the Zappos culture. Each employee, from a warehouse worker to a director, has to go through what Christa Foley, the Senior Manager of Human Resources at Zappos, calls "boot camp." For four weeks each employee is brought up to speed on how the company works, but also on how the company's culture works. It is really the second screening within the Zappos hiring process. Even after getting the job offer, you have to prove that you can absorb the culture.

The results, says Foley, are remarkable. "Those connections [employees] made during boot camp stay with them throughout their careers." Boot camp is purposefully intense—people have to show up at 7:00 a.m., work hard, meet deadlines, and pass tests. But it works. People who go through boot camp stay connected, not just for months but for years, organizing their own reunions and barbecues to stay in touch.

"It becomes an extended family," says Zappos executive Rachel Brown. "You take your work friends home with you. You hang out with them."

Another way that Zappos keeps people happy is by giving employees a chance to learn and grow. The company almost always prefers to hire internally. Say a job in HR is posted, and someone in accounting, who has always thought he might like that kind of work, sees it. That person who is curious about HR might then be brought into an "apprenticeship." It gives the employee the chance to see if he really does like that work, and it gives the manager a chance to see if he'd make a good fit with the team. The company also offers free classes taught by other employees—Finance 101, Coding for Beginners, whatever. Zappos wants people to grow at and within the company.

As I mentioned in chapter three, on teams, people want to grow; they want to get better at what they're doing and find what else they can get better at. The idea is that mastering work motivates people. Giving people the chance to find out where they fit helps Zappos keep employees happy, excited, and engaged.

For many who've plugged along in a very traditional career, this culture can be a breath of fresh air. "All of my career before

Zappos I was mostly focused on recruiting," says Foley. It was a rote job, she says, and she was burned out. Coming to Zappos reinvigorated her. It was the culture, she says. "It's what makes me excited coming to work."

That's what Zappos wants, what any company should want. It's what I want. I want people to love coming to work. It's a change in mind-set. From working for a company to working with *my* company. It's a mind-set that some people have a problem embracing. It's why Zappos focuses on internal promotions. They've found that people who come in from the outside, especially at more senior levels, have a hard time adjusting. "We're a mix of entrepreneurial and innovative," says Foley. But that's only half of it. "The other half is collaboration." The company wants people to work together in relationships across the organization. This doesn't fit sometimes with standard corporate culture. One senior manager told me, "I don't really have a title. We think as a group we can do much better."

Often at companies you'll see managers who want to run their own area without transparency, and without collaboration. They create an "us versus them" dynamic. Turf lines are drawn, and you can almost see the different divisions plotting against one another like something out of a Machiavellian medieval court. Imagine how much more productive a company would be if everyone worked together toward a common goal. Imagine a company that everyone thinks of as *my* company, where every day is a chance to get better, to do something better, to learn something new. Instead, most corporations set up an environment where people are more involved in politics than in making a profit.

At Zappos if you don't fit with the team, and the culture, you don't fit in the company. Their annualized attrition rate is 12 percent, and most of the turnover, they say, is in their call center.

That's because they fire people who aren't passionate about delivering for customers. Zappos sees those people as the public face of the company, and its standards are high. Folks at Zappos are flexible on a lot of things, but not on that.

I've seen this same dynamic play out on teams. One person on a team might have specialized knowledge or skills—knowledge they hoard like misers. They see it as a possession that ensures their job. Scrum, through its Retrospectives and transparency, illuminates this kind of behavior almost immediately. It becomes obvious where the roadblocks are, where the waste is. When I run a company, I tell those people with "miser" habits that they don't have the luxury of holding the team and the company hostage. They can either change their mind-set or go work for someone else.

Zappos has found that, the more senior the new hire, the more ingrained their thinking, and, therefore, the harder they have to work to shed old ways of doing things. Scrum gives people a framework for doing that. It provides a structure for the whole organization to head toward a common goal. Its pillars are transparency, teamwork, and collaboration. Many companies now embrace that philosophy, and inevitably those that don't lose out to those that do.

Zappos went from $1.6 million in sales in 2000, to over a billion in 2008. That's a growth rate of 124 percent each year for eight years in a row. I don't know about you, but I think that's a pretty convincing argument for making people happy. And Scrum is a tool kit you can use to get there.

Pop the Happy Bubble

One thing happiness is not—at least the kind *I'm* talking about—is complacency. Rather, it's the opposite of that: positive and passionate engagement. As Christa Foley at Zappos says, happiness is the farthest thing from passivity. "I love coming to work. Rather than [encouraging you to become] complacent, our positive and uplifting culture makes you work harder." They do have to screen out people who think that working at a happy place means not working. They want people who use joy as a driver.

And they aren't alone in that. The *Harvard Business Review* focused its entire 2012 January–February issue on happiness. What they found was

> . . . that the only route to employee happiness that also benefits shareholders is through a sense of fulfillment resulting from an important job done well. We should aspire not just to make employees "happy," but to do so by helping them achieve great things. In short, we should earn our employees' passionate advocacy for the company's mission and success by helping them earn the passionate advocacy of customers.[2]

And that passionate advocacy has tangible benefits. Happy employees show up at work, they bear down harder, and not only do they not leave a company, they attract others like them who share the same drive. In their article for the *HBR* issue, Gretchen Spreitzer and Christine Porath decided not to call these people "happy," because of the connotations of complacency. Instead, they called them "thriving." They found that these people performed 16 percent better than their peers, had 125 percent less burnout, were

32 percent more committed, and 46 percent more satisfied with their jobs. They took fewer sick days, had fewer doctor's appointments, and were more likely to get promoted.[3]

What these "thrivers" share is what I've been writing about throughout this chapter—each thriver is vital and passionate, and each is trying to perfect their craft, whether they belong to an airplane crew or are a busboy in a restaurant. What can companies do to create an atmosphere in which people thrive? Managers can encourage autonomy by letting people make their own decisions about their job. And they can make sure that employees know everything that's going on, because, as they put it, "Doing your job in an information vacuum is tedious and uninspiring." Managers should also have zero tolerance for incivility and never allow an employee to poison corporate culture through abuse or disrespect. And, finally, they should give quick and direct feedback.

Scrum gives people all those things. It's set up to *make* them happen, especially the direct feedback, which happens every day in the Daily Stand-up meeting, and which is what the Sprint Retrospective and the Happiness Metric are designed to illuminate.

There's one caution I'd like to lay out, though. It's possible— heck, it happens often enough that I've spent significant time studying it—for a "happy bubble" to develop. This usually happens after a team has achieved some big success or increased their productivity greatly by using Scrum. They've self-organized, and they feel proud of their progress. And that's when complacency can set in. They say to themselves, *Hey, we've improved so much, we don't need to improve any more.* They hit a productivity plateau and pretty soon thereafter cease to do great work. But they're good enough that, for a time, they live in this happy bubble that insulates them from unpleasant truths. They don't realize that continuous improvement means just that: it never, ever stops. When I was a fighter pilot we used to say after three thousand hours in the cockpit you need to quit because you become complacent, and that could kill you. While a complacent team might be less risky in business, ongoing team performance is at risk.

This complacent attitude often reveals itself with a comment such as the following: "We *deserve* to coast; we've earned it." Or individual team members value their team spirit and happiness so highly that they don't want to endanger it. Or they fear change itself, feeling that if what they have is working, why alter it?

Because this is where the forms of Scrum can break down, "happy bubbles" are one of my biggest concerns. I've seen it again and again: a team might be doing all the things Scrum teaches— prioritization, single-tasking, cross-functionality, review rituals— but they've stopped improving. Often they're so much better than they were before learning Scrum, and they have the successes to prove it, but they rest on their laurels. They say, "We don't *need* to get any better."

It reminds me of the 2004 US Olympic basketball team. There were some top players on that team—LeBron James, Tim Duncan, and Allen Iverson, to name just a few—and the United States had a history of not only winning but dominating in the sport, particularly since professional players had been allowed to participate. The American basketball players knew they were the best. Except that they *weren't*. They lost more games than any US Olympic basketball team had ever lost. They lost to *Lithuania*. Their pride and complacency were their downfall. They were living in the happy bubble.

So how do you pop the bubble before your players embarrass their country on live TV in front of billions of people? The first step is being aware of the problem, which is why I want teams to measure their velocity every Sprint. I want to know what their rate of change is. If there isn't positive growth, I know we've got to bear down. And the person I depend on to do this is the Scrum Master. He or she needs to be able to see the problem and bring it up with the team. It's crucial that someone ask the hard questions. What you really want is a "Wise Fool."

> I marvel what kin thou and thy daughters are: they'll have me whipped for speaking true,
> thou'lt have me whipped for lying; and sometimes I am whipped for holding my peace.[4]

> —*King Lear,* act 1, scene 4

The "Wise Fool" is the person who asks uncomfortable questions or raises uncomfortable truths. These workers aren't always easy to have around, since they can be seen as troublemakers or not part of the team, but they need to be cultivated and used.

Perhaps the best example is one we're all familiar with—from the classic Hans Christian Andersen story "The Emperor's New Clothes." As you'll recall, there was once an emperor who adored fine clothes so much, he had a different coat for every hour of the day. If you wanted to know where he was, the first place you looked was his changing room. One day a few swindlers came to the emperor and swore that they had a secret cloth that was so fine that those people who were unfit for office were unable to see it. They demanded the finest silk but only pretended to weave it, instead "weaving" only air, the fine materials going into their bags. The emperor came to check on their progress one day and saw nothing. Remembering that the cloth was only visible to those fit for office, he praised it as the finest he'd ever seen. He asked his advisers, but they too swore up and down that it was the most wondrous material ever. On the day of delivery the swindlers carefully draped the emperor in nothing at all, to rave reviews from his court, and so the emperor decided to parade through his city, showing people the miraculous cloth.

You remember how the story ends: No one said anything about the emperor's nakedness, not wanting to be seen as unfit themselves. So the royal procession continued down the avenue until a small child called out, "But he isn't wearing anything at all!" At first the child's father hushed him, but then, beginning with a whisper and growing to a shout, the people of the city started shouting, "He hasn't got anything on!" The emperor, while fearing they were right, kept the procession going. And his courtiers followed him, holding a train that wasn't there.

The Wise Fool is that child—the person who can see that the accepted truth is simply a consensual illusion, and that really the emperor has no clothes. So if you have a Wise Fool or two, cherish them.

There are other ways of popping the happy bubble—for example, by bringing in new blood and management intervention—but at the root they're all the same, bringing the team face-to-face with a reality they may not want to see. Fortunately, with Scrum everything is transparent—how much the team is producing, the quality of their work, how happy the customer is. One of Scrum's virtues is that it makes the uncomfortable visible, quickly. By contrast, traditional teams and organizations can blithely walk themselves off a cliff and wonder what possibly could have gone wrong. They wait too long to get actionable feedback from the market, and from each other.

Happy Today, Happy Tomorrow

Psychologists, including Harvard's Ben-Shahar, say that one way to analyze how people approach the world is by asking whether what they're doing makes them happy today, and whether it will make them happier tomorrow. I've found it a useful lens to look at people in work environments.

People tend to fall into four types according to Ben-Shahar. The first type, the "Hedonist," is someone who is doing what makes them happy right now. Tomorrow? *Let tomorrow worry about tomorrow. I'll just enjoy today.* I see this kind of behavior a lot in start-ups: a bunch of people in the figurative garage just making stuff, because it's cool and it's fun. But there isn't a lot of attention paid to creating a sustainable product. Very little mental energy is channeled into how this thing will be working in a month, let alone a year down the road.

And what usually happens is that the investors in these guys get worried. So they hire a bunch of managers to ride herd on the hackers. And, suddenly, the hackers find that the world they enjoyed so much now sucks. There are now all sorts of rules and tests and reports. It sucks today, and they think it will suck forever. Call them now the "Nihilists."

Then there are the guys who were brought in to run the place. They're the ones willing to put in eighty-hour weeks (and willing to whip *others* to do so), because they think they'll get promoted later, and they'll be happier. Of course, when they do get promoted, they just have a new set of headaches to contend with that require more time. They enjoy the rat race.

The fourth type of person is the one that Scrum tries to identify and encourage—the individual who is working at stuff that is fun today but has an eye toward a better future and who is convinced it will be fun forever. This sort of person rarely experiences burnout or disillusionment. He's spared the negative feelings toward work suffered by the hedonists, the nihilists, and the rat-race-addicted managers who strive to make everybody toe the line.

What Scrum does is promote a single, galvanizing mind-set. By having everyone work together, the team helps the hedonist look ahead, convinces the nihilist there is a future without whining, and tells those managers stuck in an unending rat race that there actually is a better way.

That's why I implemented the Happiness Metric in my company. It helps the team help its members become better people. It removes the causes of unhappiness systematically, carefully, and incrementally. It empowers people to change themselves and attaches an incentive to doing so.

Remember the Fundamental Attribution Error? When you're surrounded by assholes, don't look for bad people; look for bad systems that reward them for acting that way. Then you use the Happiness Metric to fix it.

In high school or college many of us studied the American psychologist Abraham Maslow's "hierarchy of needs." It laid out, in pyramid form, the needs that humans take care of first and then those that become more pressing as lower ones are satisfied. At the pyramid's base are physiological needs: air, water, food, clothing, and shelter. If we don't have those, we can't even begin to think about anything else. The next layer is safety—not just physical and financial, but also the assurance of good health. It's important to have some access to medical care. Interestingly, many people stop there, even though the next layer holds what we absolutely need as humans but that society often ignores: love and belonging—that connectedness Zappos talks about. Above that is the need for self-esteem and respect from others. And at the pyramid's very top is the need to achieve one's full potential.

It's that top layer that Maslow was most interested in, and that Scrum focuses on: helping people achieve personal growth and fulfillment. People high up on that pyramid are not only happier and more fulfilled, they're more effective and innovative. And they're able to deliver greatness.

I can almost see you nodding now, because we all know that pyramid on a gut level, even if some of us have never seen it spelled out. The trick is to move up to those lofty heights, and to then have a way of *precisely* gauging what impact you're having. If you're running a business, maybe you measure greatness by revenue and growth. If you're trying to make sick people better, maybe you measure greatness by the number of those who don't die. If you're trying to change the world, maybe you measure greatness by how *much* you've changed it. If you're just trying to get your honey-do list done, maybe you measure greatness by how many weekend afternoons you have free to go fishing.

It's not enough just to be happy. Happiness needs to be harnessed to produce results. All the elements of Scrum come together to help a person do just that. The real trick? Priorities. We will talk about those next.

THE TAKEAWAY

It's the Journey, Not the Destination. True happiness is found in the process, not the result. Often we only reward results, but what we *really* want to reward is people striving toward greatness.

Happy Is the New Black. It helps you make smarter decisions. Plus, when you're happy, you're more creative, less likely to leave your job, and more likely to accomplish far more than you ever anticipated.

Quantify Happiness. It's not enough just to feel good; you need to measure that feeling and compare it to actual performance. Other metrics look backward. Happiness is a future-looking metric.

Get Better Every Day—and Measure It. At the end of each Sprint, the team should pick one small improvement, or *kaizen,* that will make them happier. And that should become the most important thing they'll accomplish in the next Sprint.

Secrecy Is Poison. Nothing should be secret. Everyone should know everything, and that includes salaries and financials. Obfuscation only serves people who serve themselves.

Make Work Visible. Have a board that shows all the work that needs to be done, what is being worked on, and what is actually done. Everyone should see it, and everyone should update it every day.

Happiness Is Autonomy, Mastery, and Purpose. Everyone wants to control their own destiny, get better at what they do, and serve a purpose greater than themselves.

Pop the Happy Bubble. Don't get so happy that you start believing your own bullshit. Make sure happiness is measured against performance, and if there is a disconnect, be prepared to act. Complacency is the enemy of success.

CHAPTER EIGHT

Priorities

I first met Scott Maxwell at Johnny's Luncheonette in Newton Center a few years ago. I've told you about him before. He's the founder of OpenView Venture Partners, and he's the one who figured out that working longer hours creates more work than it accomplishes. I've been working with OpenView and its portfolio companies for almost eight years now, and in every single one we've seen dramatic increases in productivity. But Scrum isn't just about making teams go faster. It's about boosting impact, which, in the case of the VC guys, takes a simple form: revenue. If a company isn't making money, you don't have a successful venture; you have a hobby.

I can't tell you how many companies I've seen with great ideas and a really cool product—something that gets everyone excited, that seems to fill a market niche, that just seems as if it *should* be successful. It's just so cool. But despite megadoses of imagination, inspiration, and hard work, the people making the product can never figure out how to actually make money with it.

What's the difference between a Pets.com and a Zappos? They

both saw a market segment that people spend billions of dollars a year on. They both saw a way to deliver products more easily and cheaply online. One became emblematic of dot-com excess and the squandering of millions and millions of dollars; the other company is worth more than a billion dollars. They both had vision—what Pets.com *didn't* have was a sense of priorities. They didn't know what to do when.

I like to show people this Venn diagram.

THE PRODUCT OWNER MUST BALANCE MULTIPLE PRODUCT ATTRIBUTES

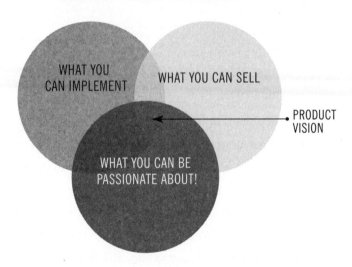

WHAT YOU CAN IMPLEMENT

WHAT YOU CAN SELL

PRODUCT VISION

WHAT YOU CAN BE PASSIONATE ABOUT!

Every company needs to think about this diagram. If you concentrate only on what you can build, you can end up making something that nobody actually wants, even if you're passionate about it. If you concentrate only on what you can sell, you can promise things you can't build. If you only build what you can sell but aren't passionate about, you end up working hard to build mediocrity. But in the center, that sweet spot, is a vision rooted in reality—a vision with a real possibility of becoming something great. In this chapter

I'm going to show you how to get there. The preceding chapters have focused on how to do things faster and better. This chapter is how to make "faster and better" work for you—how to achieve greatness.

Scott Maxwell says that the true power of Scrum lies in its ready, prioritized, and sized Backlog of what to do. This is why he implemented it at the venture group, and why he thinks it is a critical competitive advantage.

The Backlog: What to Do When

The first thing you need to do when you're implementing Scrum is to create a Backlog. It can be hundreds of items long, or contain only the few things that you need to figure out first. Of course, you need a clear idea of what you want at the end of the work. It could be a product, a wedding, a service, a new vaccine, or a house painted. It could be anything, but once you have a vision, you need to consider what it will take to make that happen.

There's a company I've been working with recently that builds automation systems for buildings—heating, cooling, electric, plumbing, the whole kit and caboodle. One of their new products is a home automation system. They're building a system that can control every aspect of your home, from opening the front door, to controlling your heating costs, to turning on your lights—all from your mobile device. So they sat down and wrote out a list of everything they would need to make that happen—switches, controllers, interfaces, sensors, communication protocols, whatever. Not the specific rules and pieces, actually, but all the "stories" they would need.

So they wrote things such as, "As a home owner, I want to be able to see who is at my door, so that I can open the door only for those people I want to come in." They wrote stories about opening the garage door, turning on the HVAC, controlling the lights. They kept writing until they had a list of all the things they thought their system would need to do to be a compelling purchase.

The list turned out to be hundreds of items long. It's a big, complicated system. The idea behind the Backlog is that it should have everything that could possibly be included in the product. You're never going to actually build it all, but you want a list of everything that *could* be included in that product vision.

The key, though, is what you decide to do first. The questions you need to ask are: what are the items that have the biggest business impact, that are most important to the customer, that can make the most money, and are the easiest to do? You have to realize that there are a whole bunch of things on that list that you will never get to, but you want to get to the things that deliver the most value with the lowest risk first. With Scrum's incremental development and delivery, you want to begin with the things that will immediately create revenue, effectively "de-risking" the project. And you want to do that on the features level. You want to start delivering value to your customers as soon as you possibly can. You want something that is completely Done—that you can show. It could be just a small part of the larger project, but it should be demonstrably Done. If you're painting a house, maybe what's Done first is all the trim in the living room.

In product development there's a hard-and-fast rule that has been proven over and over again. I talked about this earlier: 80 percent of the value is in 20 percent of the features. Think about that for a moment. In anything that you buy, most of the value—most of what people want—is in only a fifth of what has been built. In this company's case they looked at this huge list of things that could be included in their home automation system, and they knew—they *knew*—that customers really only wanted 20 percent of them. The trick of Scrum is figuring out how you build that 20 percent first. In traditional product development, teams don't know what that 20 percent is until they deliver the whole thing. That means that fully 80 percent of their effort is waste. And you know how I feel about waste.

What if you could start delivering things five times faster than your competition, with five times the value? That's a winning hand.

So this automation company sat down with a huge list of features and asked themselves: "Okay, what do we do tomorrow? What's most important to the customer? How do we deliver value to them faster than anyone else?" As Scott Maxwell says, the difficult part isn't figuring out *what* you want to accomplish; it's figuring out what you *can* accomplish. This is true whether you're building a house or car, writing a book or videogame, or cleaning up crime or trash. Figure out where the most value can be delivered for the least effort, and do that one right away. Then identify the next increment of value, and the next. Faster than you think, you'll have created something or delivered something with demonstrable, real results. The key is prioritizing the work.

How do you do that? Well, first you need someone who can figure out both what the vision is, and where the value lies. In Scrum we call that person the Product Owner.

The Product Owner

There are only three roles in Scrum. Either you're part of the team, and you're doing the work, or you're a Scrum Master, helping the team figure out how to do the work better, or you're a Product Owner. This is all laid out in the appendix. The Product Owner decides what the work should be. He or she owns the Backlog, what's on it, and, most important, what order it's in.

When I started the first Scrum team in 1993, I didn't have a Product Owner. I was part of the leadership team and had a bunch of other responsibilities besides figuring out exactly what the team should do in each Sprint. I carried out management and marketing duties, dealt with customers, and plotted strategy. But in that first Sprint I figured I could handle the Backlog. I just needed to make sure I had enough "stories" and features for the team to work on during the next Sprint. The problem was, after the second Sprint we introduced the Daily Stand-up meeting. Velocity went up 400 percent in the *next* Sprint, and the team finished in a week what we thought would take us a month. There was no more Backlog for them to work on! I thought I'd have a month to create more "stories." A great problem to have, admittedly, but one that had to be addressed. So I thought about this role of Product Owner and what qualities someone would need to execute it properly.

My inspiration for the role came from Toyota's Chief Engineer. A Chief Engineer at Toyota is responsible for a whole product line, such as the Corolla or the Camry. To do this, they have to draw on the talents of groups specializing in body engineering, or chassis, or electrical, or whatever. The Chief Engineer has to draw from all those groups to create a cross-functional team capable of creating a car. Outside of Toyota everyone thinks of these legendary Chief Engineers (or *Shusas*, as they were originally called) as all-powerful leaders of the "Toyota Way." And in a way they are. But what they don't have is authority. No one reports to them—rather, they report to their own groups. People can tell Chief Engineers that they're wrong, so they have to make sure they're right. They don't give anyone performance appraisals or promotions or raises. But they do decide on the vision of the car, and how the car will be made—by persuasion, not coercion.

It's this idea that I wanted to embody within Scrum. John Shook of the Lean Enterprise Institute once began his description of the Chief Engineer role by quoting the US Marine Corps leadership manual:

> An individual's responsibility for leadership is not dependent on authority. . . . the deep-rooted assumption that authority should equal responsibility is the root of much organizational evil. I believe misunderstanding around this issue is rampant, problematic, and runs so deep in our consciousness that we don't even realize it.[1]

Reflecting on my time at West Point and in Vietnam, I found myself agreeing that leadership has nothing to do with authority. Rather, it has to do with—among other things—knowledge and being a servant-leader. The Chief Engineer can't simply *say* something has to be done a particular way. He has to persuade, cajole, and demonstrate that his way is the right way, the *best* way. It usually takes someone with thirty years of experience to fill the role. I wanted that in Scrum, but I'm also well aware that very few people have that level of skill and experience. So I split the role in two, giving the Scrum Master the *how* and the Product Owner the *what*.

Even in those early days of Scrum I knew that I needed someone who was deeply connected to the customer. The Product Owner needed to be able to deliver feedback to the team from the customer each and every Sprint. They needed to spend half their time talking to the people buying the product (getting their thoughts on the latest incremental release and how it delivered value) and half their time with the team creating the Backlog (showing them what the customers valued and what they didn't).

Remember, the "customer" could be the general consumer, a big bank, your husband, or someone who needs the rotavirus vaccine and is depending on you to get it to them. The customer is anyone who will get value from what you're doing.

But I didn't want a manager. I wanted someone the team would believe and trust when he prioritized the Backlog. So I went and got the smartest guy in Product Marketing—not in Engineering, mind you, but Marketing. And that's how Don Rodner became the first Product Owner. He knew the product we were making not from a technical point of view—although he understood enough of that to communicate with the engineers—but, rather, from a customer point of view. What did the people who were actually using the product need? When you're picking a Product Owner, get someone who can put themselves in the mind of whoever is getting value from what you're doing. As a friend of mine says, "My wife is the perfect Product Owner; she knows exactly what she wants. I just implement it."

Not only does the Product Owner need a wider range of skills than a Scrum Master, they need to be held to a different set of standards. The Scrum Master and the team are responsible for how fast they're going and how much faster they can get. The Product Owner is accountable for translating the team's productivity into value.

Over the years I've boiled down the essential characteristics of a Product Owner to four:

One, the Product Owner needs to be knowledgeable about the domain. By this I mean two things: the Product Owner should understand the process the team is executing well enough to know what can be done and, just as important, what can't. But the Product Owner also has to understand the *what* well enough to know how to translate what can be done into true, meaningful value. It could be a computer system that helps the FBI catch terrorists, or a teaching method that improves student performance in public schools. The Product Owner needs to know the market well enough to know what will make a difference.

Two, the Product Owner has to be empowered to make decisions. Just as management shouldn't interfere with the team, the Product Owner should be given the leeway to make decisions about what the product vision will be, and what needs to be done to get there. This is important, because the Product Owner is under pressure from a lot of different stakeholders, both internal and external, and has to be able to hold firm. The Product Owner should be responsible for outcomes, but let the team make their own decisions.

Three, the Product Owner has to be available to the team, to explain what needs to be done and why. While the Product Owner is ultimately accountable for the Backlog, there needs to be a constant dialogue with the team. Often the team's expertise will inform the decisions the Product Owner needs to make. The Product Owner has to be reliable, consistent, and available. Without access to him, the team won't know what to do, or what order to do it in. They rely on the Product Owner for "the vision" and, also, market intelligence on what is important. If the Product Owner isn't available to the team, the whole process can fall apart. This is one of the reasons I rarely recommend that CEOs or other senior executives be Product Owners. They just don't have the time the team needs.

Four, the Product Owner needs to be accountable for value.

In a business context what matters is revenue. I measure a Product Owner by how much revenue they deliver per "point" of effort. If the team is producing forty points of work every week, I want to measure how much revenue is created for each and every point. But the measurement of value could be how many successes a team has. I know one law enforcement team that measured value by the number of arrests of wanted felons they made each week. I know churches that use Scrum and measure their success by how well they're serving their congregation, and whether it's growing. The key is to decide what the measure of value is and hold the Product Owner accountable for delivering more of it. In Scrum this kind of metric is easy to observe because of the method's incredible transparency.

Now, that's a lot to ask of one person, and it's the reason why in big projects there's usually a *team* of Product Owners to address all the needs. I'll get into the details of that later. But first, as a way of visualizing what the Product Owner needs to do, I want you to imagine you're in the cockpit of an F-86 Sabre with the "Mad Major," John Boyd, about to enter a dogfight over the Korean Peninsula.

Observe, Orient, Decide, Act

Air-to-air combat during the Korean War took place mainly between American F-86 Sabres and Russian-made MiG-15s. The MiG was faster, more maneuverable, had a greater thrust-to-weight ratio, and was all around a superior aircraft. On paper, MiG-15s should have wiped the skies of American pilots. Instead, they were shot down by a 10:1 ratio. The struggle to figure out how that could possibly happen shaped the future of warfare; it also became critical in the development of Scrum.

John Boyd was simply the greatest fighter pilot who ever lived, although he never shot down an enemy in combat. He flew only twenty-two missions over Korea before the armistice, and back then you had to have thirty missions as a wingman before you could take the lead as a "shooter." It was after the war, teaching at the USAF Weapons School at Nellis Air Force Base in southern Nevada, that he made his mark. In a military that values frequent rotations of personnel, he spent an unprecedented six years there as an instructor.

Fighter pilots are not a humble lot. By the time they show up at Nellis, they're already considered the best pilots in the USAF, and they exhibit a certain swagger. Boyd had a foolproof way of dismantling a pilot's ego so he would actually learn what Boyd had to teach. He'd invite them up into the air and have the student fly on his "six," directly behind him—the best position in an aerial dogfight. Then he'd tell the student to engage. Without fail, within forty seconds he'd be lining up a kill shot on the student's six, all the while screaming "Guns! Guns! Guns!" into the radio. This was before the advent of lasers and computers and simulated weapons. It was that yell that told the student he was dead. Boyd's unfailing success earned him a second nickname that would stay with him, "Forty Second" Boyd.

His other sobriquet, the "Mad Major," was a moniker earned from his, ah, energetic declarations. They were almost always delivered with his face three inches from whoever was contradicting him while he poked the opponent's chest with two fingers. Unfailingly, in those two fingers was a lit Dutch Masters cigar. Legend had it that, occasionally—quite by accident, I'm sure—he'd light his adversary's tie on fire. At such times, he'd show no contrition, using any weapon in his arsenal to win an argument.

Boyd had the ability to see the whole battle space. As he put it in an oral history:

> I would see myself in a vast ball—I would be *inside* the ball—and I could visualize all the actions taking place around the ball [while] all the time of course I am maneuvering. . . . I could visualize from two reference points. When I was fighting air-to-air, *I could see myself as a detached observer looking at myself, plus all the others around me.*[2]

This kind of awareness, the ability to see a whole sphere of sky and watch events unfold, shaped his military theories and eventually rewrote how America wages war.

When Boyd left Weapons School, he decided to study engineering, and while doing so he created a model of aircraft performance that described air-to-air combat in terms of energy relationships. Energy Maneuverability (EM) theory takes into account an airplane's kinetic and potential energies in any situation—its altitude, airspeed, and direction—and how fast it can change any of those variables. The theory was eventually baked into the way most fighter aircraft are modeled, directly leading to the development of the F-15 and the F-16, the dominant fighters of the last forty years.

The problem was, according to Boyd's theory, the MiG-15 should have wiped the floor with the F-86 Sabre. It just didn't make sense. Boyd, according to Robert Coram's biography, went into frequent trances for days as he tried to figure it out. He was sure his theory was right, but what was the reason for the 10:1 kill ratio racked up by American pilots? Training? That could only explain part of it. Tactics? Maybe, but again that factor wouldn't lead to so lopsided a result. And then it hit him. The American pilots could see better and act faster. Not through any quality inherent in the pilots, but through some simple design choices. The Sabre had a bubble canopy, while the MiG had one with multiple glass panes and struts blocking the pilot's vision. The F-86 also had fully hydraulically powered flight controls, while the MiG had only hydraulically *assisted* controls. MiG-15 pilots were known to lift weights to give themselves the upper body strength to maneuver the aircraft.

As a result the American pilots could see the MiGs first, and then, crucially, they could act on that information faster than the Chinese and North Korean pilots. The battle was decided not by what the machine could do, but by how fast observation was translated into action. The MiG would take one action, the American pilot would respond, and while the MiG pilot was trying to respond to that, the American pilot could take another action. He'd respond to each new alignment of the MiG so much faster that the more technologically advanced plane became a sitting duck.

The same phenomenon occurred in Vietnam when I was there. By then, there were different airplanes squaring off, the MiG-21 and the F-4, but, once again, the superior visibility of the F-4 overcame the superior maneuverability of the Soviet-made plane. As Boyd would put it, his most famous innovation put pilots "inside the enemy's decision loop."

This insight has become fundamental to how wars are fought. And it's exactly what I designed Scrum for—to allow a Product Owner to make decisions quickly, based on real-time feedback. By getting constant input from whoever is getting value from what you're doing—be it the person clicking the Buy button on Amazon, the parishioners of your church, the children in a classroom, or someone trying on a dress—you're in a position to constantly adjust your strategy and more quickly succeed.

The idea goes by the somewhat ludicrous name of the OODA

loop. That's short for **O**bserve, **O**rient, **D**ecide, and **A**ct. And while it may sound funny on the tongue, it's deadly in war and in business. Getting inside someone's loop reduces them to confusion and doubt. They overreact and underreact. As Boyd put it in a briefing he gave to other officers, "He who can handle the quickest rate of change survives."[3] See the OODA loop chart on page 185.

"Observe" is fairly obvious—it's clearly seeing the situation as it unfolds. This isn't as simple as it sounds, though. Boyd described it as moving outside of yourself so as to see the whole picture—not merely your own point of view.

"Orient" is not just about where you are; it's also about what outcomes you're capable of seeing—the menu of alternatives you create for yourself. Factoring into that creation, according to Boyd, are genetic heritage, cultural traditions, previous experiences, and, of course, the unfolding circumstances. Thus, Orientation reflects not only how you see the world and your place in it, but what world you're *capable* of seeing.

The combination of Observation and Orientation leads to a "Decision," which leads to "Action." Then the loop begins again with Observation of the results of your actions and those of your opponent—or, in the business world, Observation of the reaction of the marketplace.

What Scrum does, by delivering a working increment, is give the Product Owner the ability to see how much value that increment creates, how people react to it. Then, based on that information, she can change what the team will do in the next Sprint. This sets up a constant feedback cycle that accelerates innovation and adaptation, and enables the Product Owner to measure how much value is delivered. (In business we measure that by money. If I'm painting the interior of a house, I might measure it by rooms com-

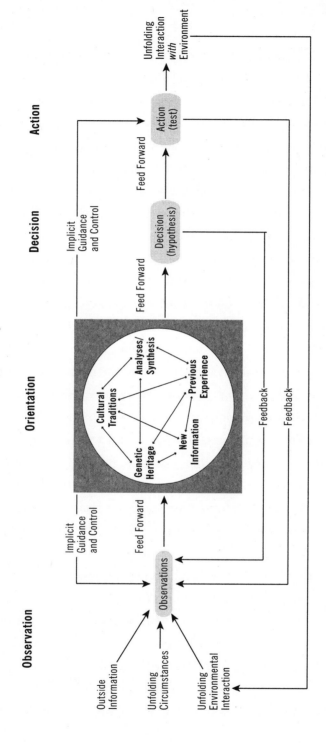

OODA Loop

Observation | Orientation | Decision | Action

Outside Information

Unfolding Circumstances

Unfolding Environmental Interaction

Observations

Implicit Guidance and Control

Feed Forward

Cultural Traditions

Analyses/ Synthesis

Previous Experience

Genetic Heritage

New Information

Feed Forward

Feedback

Feedback

Implicit Guidance and Control

Decision (hypothesis)

Feed Forward

Action (test)

Unfolding Interaction *with* Environment

pleted.) The Product Owner thus has the ability to adjust on the fly to a constantly changing world.

It can be difficult to imagine incremental releases on products or projects that don't seem, on the face of it, to have any value until they're complete. For example, how do you do incremental releases of a car? Or a hundred-million-dollar video game? The key is to look for what slices actually hold value—enough value that you can get real feedback on them and react in real time.

Let's take cars, for example. Toyota developed the Prius from concept to delivery in fifteen months, faster than any delivery they'd ever done. While the team that designed and built the Prius didn't start selling their car before it was completed, they did start rapidly prototyping the car so that the Chief Engineer could "kick the tires" and see if the team was going in the right direction. This kind of rapid prototyping—making fully functional vehicles before release and then improving those prototypes over and over until you have the product you want to sell to consumers—can drive incredibly fast changes. The key is not to have a fully established design at the beginning but, rather, to make a functional prototype, then see what you can improve. And then, having improved it, to make the next prototype and improve that one. The idea is that the sooner you have some real feedback, the faster you can make a better car.

Team WIKISPEED, which I wrote about in chapter four, produces full prototypes of their car every *week*. And they sell those prototypes. These transactions don't occur in a mass market—Team WIKISPEED isn't ready for that yet—but there *are* early adopters who are willing to put down $25,000 for those early prototypes. When you're thinking about building something, don't assume you can't deliver something of value until the very end. Instead, try to think about the minimum viable product. *What is the absolute least I can build and still deliver some value to a customer?*

Videogames are another good example. Nowadays more and more developers are letting early adopters pay for early "alpha" access. That way the developers get feedback from their most dedicated fans before the game really works. This allows them to see how people actually react, rather than guess how they will react.

Depending on the industry you're a part of, or the organization you run, it can be difficult to wrap your head around this idea of incremental releases. A fallback, if you can't put something before an *external* customer, is to identify an *internal* customer—for example, the Product Owner—who can act in lieu of the public. Show your internal customer whatever will elicit useful feedback: bits and pieces of a real-estate expansion plan, a factory-upgrade design, a braking-system rebuild, a volunteer service campaign— whatever. The idea is to create for yourself an opportunity to inspect and adapt. A company or organization that can't react to changing conditions, competitors, or tastes is in trouble.

Boyd puts it this way:

> We want to get inside another guy's tempo or rhythm, where we will pull him down. . . . We gotta get an image or picture in our head, which we call orientation. Then we have to make a decision as to what we're going to do, and then implement the decision. . . . Then we look at the [resulting] action, plus our observation, and we drag in new data, new orientation, new decision, new action, ad infinitum. . . . Orientation isn't just a state you're in; it's a process. You're always orienting. . . .
>
> A nice tight little world where there's no change . . . [creatures who live in such a world are] dinosaurs; they're going to die.

> The name of the game is not to become a dinosaur. If you're in an equilibrium condition, you're dead. . . . The underlying message is simple: there is no way out. . . . That's the way it is, guys.[4]

That's the way it is, guys. As I said in chapter one, there's a pretty stark choice in front of you: change or die. If you don't get inside your competition's decision loop, they'll get inside yours. As Boyd said, "What I want to do is fold my adversary back inside himself. . . . Then I can drive him into confusion and disorder and bring about paralysis." I don't know about you, but me, I'd rather be on the doing end of that than the receiving end.

First Things First

So you have a Product Owner who's constantly updating the Backlog, ordering the stuff to be built and delivered. When you have a few hundred items, that ordering process can get pretty complex pretty fast. The key is to figure out how to deliver the most value the most quickly. There may be many millions of ways to arrange that Backlog, but the one you want delivers those 20 percent of features that hold 80 percent of the value as quickly as possible. Your first guess for the first Sprint almost certainly won't be the right one, but it will be your best guess at the time.

But that's just your first guess. After the first Sprint, once you've completed the OODA loop and delivered some product to customers, you'll change that order, realizing that another arrangement is actually better.

And then you keep doing it, continually updating and re-prioritizing the Backlog each Sprint, tacking toward the order that delivers value the fastest. You'll probably never reach the absolute perfect order, but you want to move toward it step by step, Sprint by Sprint.

The key thing to remember is that the order is always in flux. The right order one week won't be the same the next. Your environment will have changed. You'll have learned new things. You'll have discovered that some things are easier and some harder. So this constant shifting of the Backlog order happens every single Sprint. The key is to acknowledge uncertainty, to fully accept that your current snapshot of order and value is only relevant at that one particular moment. It'll change again. And again. And again.

One bad habit a company can fall into, because of constantly shifting market needs and because managers don't know exactly where the most value lies, is prioritizing everything. Everything is *top priority*. The adage to keep in mind comes from Frederick II of Prussia, later to be called "the Great": "He who will defend everything defends nothing." By not concentrating both your resources and your mental energies, you thin them out to irrelevancy.

A few years ago I celebrated my seventieth birthday in Normandy in France. I went to see the famous beach where my own father had landed during the D-day invasion. At low tide, Omaha Beach looks as if it slopes for miles before sinking into the distant sea—a seemingly endless spread of sand. Running up that long, wet slope into the face of the German guns must have required a courage that can only be imagined. Walking through the graves of the thousands who died that day demands silence and respect. But as I started reading about the German defenses, I realized that one of the reasons the American landing was successful was that the Germans forgot Frederick the Great's admonition. So confused were they by Allied deceptions that they spread their forces across the entire coast of France. As a result, the Allies could isolate each German unit separately, defeating each and then moving on to the next. The Nazis didn't prioritize properly, and, thankfully, they lost it all.

Release

So you have the priorities. You know where 80 percent of the value lies. When do you deliver your product? Here is where Scrum can deliver value radically faster. Whenever you're making something, you want to put it in the hands of those who are actually going to use it as fast as possible. You want to do this even before you make 20 percent of the features. You want to do this with something that delivers at least a *tiny bit* of value. I call this a "Minimum Viable Product," or MVP. This should be the thing you show to the public for the first time. How effective does it have to be? Well, it should actually work, though to a person who has been working on it, it may seem kind of embarrassing. You need to get that product out to the public *as early as is feasible!* This will get you the feedback you need to power your decision loop and prioritization. This is Version 0.5. This is a camera that can take a picture but can't focus. This is a dining room set with two chairs. This is distributing a vaccine to five out of the hundred villages you're trying to help. It's almost laughably incomplete.

But what it gets you is *feedback*. The camera's body is really awkward to hold because the shutter button is in a weird place. The chair's wood doesn't match the table's closely enough. You manage to offend the village elders through a totally avoidable social faux pas. Make those mistakes early, with as little damage as possible.

Then, when you do an official release, or a rollout of a big program, you'll have already adjusted and found out what people actually value. In our camera example, maybe it turns out that picture takers *said* that having a landscape mode and being able to share photos on Facebook were equally valuable, but when they actually started *using* it, they never used the landscape mode but always wanted to post photos on Facebook.

This allows you to make the features they value, first, and release your product when you've only done about 20 percent of the work. You know it's not perfect, but it's darn close. Every hour spent polishing the apple is lost opportunity for value.

VALUE CURVE-RADICALLY *FASTER* DELIVERY

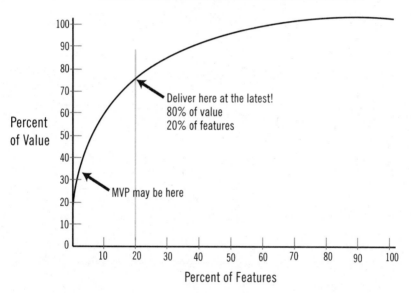

What's great about this process is that it's iterative: just "rinse and repeat." Once people have your product or service or change in their lives, they'll tell you what the *next* most valuable things are. Then develop 20 percent of that, and deliver again. And again.

With this incremental-release process, in the time it would've taken you to create half of the features of your initial product or project, you've now released 200 percent of the value, in half the time. That's the real power of Scrum. That's how it can fundamentally change not only how you work, but how you live your life. Don't focus on delivering a whole list of things—everything and the kitchen sink—focus on delivering what's valuable, what people actually want or need.

I'm reminded of stories out of Iraq or Afghanistan. They went like this: An American platoon comes into town, looks around, and

COMPOUNDING VALUE-RADICALLY *BETTER* DELIVERY

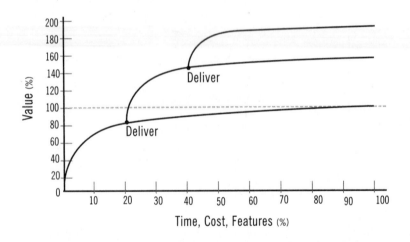

says, "These people are raising chickens. Let's build them a chicken-processing plant." So they spend millions of dollars building a state-of-the-art chicken plant. They don't consider that there's almost no regular electricity, or that the townsfolk are mostly illiterate and can't easily be trained on the equipment. Then someone comes to town and asks the villagers, "What would *really* help you?" and they say, "You know, a footbridge across the river would be great, so we don't have to spend half a day going to the nearest crossing to get to market." That footbridge costs a few hundred dollars. It looks a lot less impressive than a big plant. It doesn't sound dramatic when you talk to your bosses back in Washington. But to those townspeople, it's infinitely more valuable than the fancy building with the now-rusting machines.

Another point worth making is that sometimes you finish early. Let's say you're making a super, next-generation alarm clock for Alarm Clock Inc. You have a list with dozens of features on it: a clock, a snooze button, a timer, a loud alarm, a radio, an iPhone dock, a GPS—whatever. But being a savvy Product Owner, you prioritize what people really want: an easy-to-set-up alarm, sufficient loudness, a radio, and a display vivid enough to be seen whether the room is bright or dark. And when your team is done with that, you realize that they've actually created the most elegant alarm clock ever made. It's the Apple iPod of alarm clocks. It's beautiful and does one thing really, really well. Instead of having your team build on to it additional features, you release that clock and start work on the next project. The team can deliver more value doing something else.

Money for Nothing and Change for Free

At this book's beginning, I told you the story of the Sentinel project at the FBI. If you remember, an outsourced contractor spent hundreds of millions of dollars building software that didn't work. One of the big sources of the cost overruns there—and in just about any contract, be it to build computer software, airplanes, or buildings—is change fees. Racking up change fees is actually the business model of a bunch of government contractors. They'll underbid a project, knowing that they'll make a profit because of change orders. When a contract is written on a years-long project with all the requirements spelled out in those pretty-looking charts, it's tempting to say, "Well, that covers it." Then the contractor says, "I'm agreeing to do this and only this. *If you want any changes, it will cost you.*" This after-the-fact billing has become the center of so much cost that companies and agencies have set up Change Control Boards. From a cost point of view, it makes sense. Limit the number of changes, and you'll limit the cost associated with them.

What the bean counters don't realize is that they're setting up a system that is designed to deny people what they actually want. They're trying to limit cost, but in doing so, they're limiting learning, innovation, and creativity. If you begin a project and realize a little way in that the real value, that 20 percent, doesn't reside in the features you laid out—it lives in a different set of things you discovered in the process of doing the work—traditional project management is set up to stop you. It's set up to stop delivering value faster.

Plus, the effort to "exercise firm control" doesn't even work! Even with Change Control Boards trying to limit changes, the need for change is so great that they're often overruled. Without the changes there wouldn't be any value in the project. So, grudgingly, the Change Control Boards allow it, and the project costs more. And then there's another change that has to be done. And, whoops, there's another. And pretty soon the project is millions of dollars over budget, and a year, or two, or five years late.

That's why I came up with the idea of "Change for Free." In a standard fixed-price contract, just say changes are free. List all the functionality you expect; for example, if you're building a tank, you want one that can go seventy-five miles per hour and shoot ten rounds a minute, has seating for four, has AC, etc., etc.—everything you think you need for that tank. The builder looks at that description and says, Hmm, making that engine, I'll call that 100 points, the loading mechanism, let's call that 50, the seating, 5, etc., on down the list. At the end there is a set number of points for each feature. Then every Sprint, the customer, who in this scenario is contractually obligated to work closely with the Product Owner, can change priorities completely. Any item or feature in the Backlog can be moved anywhere else. And new features? No problem: just drop equivalently sized features from the deliverables. Oh, you want a laser-guided system now? Well, that's 50 points of work—to compensate for that addition, let's drop 50 points of low-priority features from the bottom of the Backlog.

A few companies have taken to a new level this idea of only delivering to a customer high-value features. A few years ago I heard about a Scrum developer that got a $10 million contract to deliver software for a big construction company. The two parties agreed on a twenty-month time frame. But the Scrum company inserted a clause into the contract. If the construction firm wanted to terminate at any time, they could—they'd just have to pay 20 percent of the value of the remaining contract. Basically, if the software worked the way the construction firm wanted, they could stop the Scrum shop from building any more.

The software developer started Sprinting. They did one-month Sprints. After the first month, the customer redirected some of the developer's effort to get more value. In the second month, the same thing. After the third month, the customer terminated the contract, took the software, and put it to work. They had the value they needed.

Let's do a little math here to see how everyone won. In the first three months of the contract the customer paid out $1.5 million to the Scrum firm. Terminating the contract early required them to pay 20 percent of the remaining $8.5 million—that's $1.7 million. They paid out $3.2 million for a piece of software they thought would cost $10 million, and they got it seventeen months early.

And they weren't the only winner. The Scrum company bid on the contract with an expected profit margin of 15 percent. So they spent $1.3 million on development in those first three months. But they received $3.2 million. Their profit margin went from 15 percent to 60 percent. That's a 400-percent increase in earnings. And now, with their developers idle, they could bid on other projects. That's not just good business. That's an early-retirement strategy.

They could do this because of the building blocks of Scrum. By managing themselves as a cross-functional unit, the team was able to accelerate quickly, delivering more value faster. At the end of every Sprint an increment of the product was Done. It worked. It could be deployed immediately. Each Sprint the Product Owner was able to re-prioritize the Backlog based on customer feedback. And when there was enough value created for the customer, everyone stopped working. In this way Scrum aligns everyone's interests: those of the team, the Scrum Master, the Product Owner, the customer, and the company. Everyone works toward the same goal and with the same vision: *deliver real value as fast as possible.* I'm a big believer in win-win situations, and making more money delivering better products at a lower price strikes me as a pretty good deal.

Risk

Management of risk is at the heart of any successful venture. What Scrum allows you to do is reduce the risks of failure. The three most common types are market risk, technical risk, and financial risk. Or, to put it another way: Do people want what we're building? Can we actually build it? Can we really sell what we've built?

I've written a lot about market risk. Scrum helps you minimize it by emphasizing incremental delivery. It allows you to put a product in front of customers faster. And by obtaining feedback early and often, you can make small changes on the spot rather than be forced into big changes after you've invested millions of dollars and realize that what you're building isn't really what the customer actually wants. It's often what the customer *said* they wanted at the beginning of the process, but in reality people don't know what they really want until they can try something out. A lot of business advice revolves around failing quickly. I prefer to think about delivering fast.

Technical risk is interesting. The question of whether it's actually possible to build what the customer wants is a tricky one, especially if you're making something that is physical, which requires plants and tooling and up-front investment.

Remember the company with the home automation system? Well, they approached it by doing what is called "set-based concurrent engineering." What that means in English is "building a few different prototypes to see which one works best before going into full production." For example, they knew that they needed a camera so customers could see who was knocking at their door and buzz the visitor in. The most expensive part of the camera, and the one that required the most lead time, was the lens. Should it be plastic? Glass? Crystal? What holds up in any weather? What scratches easily? What gives the clearest picture? How much does each type cost to manufacture?

Instead of making the decision up front and going full bore into manufacturing, they built three different fully functional lenses and compared them. Since they were only really trying to figure out the lens question, and they had to do it first because of long lead times in manufacturing, they tested each lens using a laptop-camera setup. Turned out, glass met the criteria the best. But, critically, they were able to make that judgment after *seeing* something that actually worked. The call wasn't based on theoretical constructs. They had something they could look at and touch. With that question answered, they could move on to designing the case that would hold the lens and the processors that would handle the image. By prioritizing that lens decision, the company potentially saved themselves millions. Apple famously does this with all their products, often building a dozen fully functioning prototypes before organizing a shoot-out to see which one is the best. This allows different ideas to be expressed quickly without a massive investment.

Financial risk is what causes most companies to fail. They've built something cool, but they can't sell it for enough to actually make a profit. A classic example of this is online journalism and the death of the newspaper. When the web first exploded in the nineties, newspapers were eager to get their content on the Internet. Some newspaper chiefs figured that, off-line or on, people would pay to advertise, so they made the content free. The problem, of course, was that advertisers were willing to pay far less money for online ads than print ads. Yet the cost of producing content remained the same. Others tried to put up pay walls in front of their content, but there were so many sites offering news for free that they were often forced to follow suit. Having actual reporters go places and witness things is expensive. You can see the results in the shuttering of newsrooms across the country.

This idea of providing content or a service for free, and then making money on the advertising, is still prevalent in tech start-ups to this day. Entrepreneurs look at Facebook or Google and say, "I can do that." The problem is that there just aren't that many Face-books and Googles. In the Internet's early days, when online space first allowed companies to target particular customer segments, "hyper-focusing" was seen as valuable. But as more and more plat-forms have arisen to facilitate it, the capability doesn't quite have the same allure.

Another way that companies fall apart financially is by over-paying to acquire customers. One example is daily-coupon com-panies such as Groupon and Living Social. At their inception, they acquired customers quickly and easily. But as they expanded their reach and built up their head count, it became more and more costly to attract additional advertisers and more people willing to buy a coupon. You can see the results in these companies' valuations.

What Scrum does for business is answer the key question fast: Will we make money making this? By putting incremental releases in front of customers quickly, you'll find out what your customers value and what they're willing to pay for. And if your first guesses were wrong, you can make changes. The most you can lose is the cost in time and energy of the few Sprints you invested—as op-posed to the multimillion-dollar cost of building a huge compli-cated infrastructure, only to find out that, while people loved your product, they didn't love it enough to pay for what it cost to make it.

Here's What You Do Tomorrow

Okay, what do you do tomorrow to implement Scrum where you work? The first step is just putting together a Backlog and a team. Think about the vision you have for your product or service or whatever, and start breaking down the things you need to do to execute that vision. You don't need a whole lot—just a week's worth of Backlog. And while the team members are holding their Daily Stand-up meetings and running their first Sprint, you'll be able to build up enough Backlog to keep the team busy for the next two Sprints. Always keep one eye on that Backlog, though, because as your team accelerates, they'll start delivering more than you thought possible.

Then, as the Product Owner, put together a road map of where you think things are going. What do you think you can get done this quarter? Where do you want to be this year? It's important to remember that this is just a snapshot in time, so don't overplan, just estimate. You're not creating a binding contract of deliverables; you're simply setting down your thoughts on where you'll be in a while. Believe me, the picture *will* change. Perhaps radically.

The reason for doing this type of planning is to create transparency within the organization. If you have a sales team, they need to know what features you're working on so they can start marketing them. Leadership needs to have some idea of where the revenue is going to come from—also, when and how much. The key message is that everything is being done in the open. Anyone can see where your product is at any time. They can see the stories move across the Scrum board to Done. They can graph story points against time on a Burndown Chart and watch a nice, steady line move toward zero, or burn down. They know how many story points your team did last Sprint, and how many you're estimating they'll do next. Know that as the Product Owner you're going to be evaluated on revenue and cost.

What you'll quickly find, especially if you're working in a place with multiple teams, is that you'll need to start putting together a Product Owner team so you can generate enough Backlog for the teams to plow through. You might have one Product Owner who focuses more on strategy and customer interaction, and another who's more tactical, deciding what the teams will be working on during each Sprint.

The important thing, though, is just to begin. Just start. You can see the detailed steps on how to do it in the appendix. Scrum is designed so that you can boot up a team in a couple of days. Get your Backlog, plan your first Sprint, and away you go. You don't need to devote a lot of time to planning, reflection, meditations, mission statements, or five-year projections. Leave all that to the competition, and let them eat your dust. And along the way, why don't you make the world a better place? In the next chapter, I'll show you how.

THE TAKEAWAY

Make a List. Check It Twice. Create a list of everything that could possibly be done on a project. Then prioritize it. Put the items with the highest value and lowest risk at the top of that Backlog, then the next, and then the next.

The Product Owner. She translates vision into Backlog. She needs to understand the business case, the market, and the customer.

A Leader Isn't a Boss. A Product Owner sets out *what* needs to be done and *why*. *How* the team accomplishes it and *who* accomplishes it is up to the team.

SCRUM

The Product Owner: Has knowledge of the domain and the power to make final decisions. He or she is available to answer questions and is accountable for delivering value.

Observe, Orient, Decide, Act (OODA). See the whole strategic picture, but act tactically and quickly.

Fear, Uncertainty, and Doubt. It's better to give than to receive. Get inside your competition's OODA loop and wrap them up in their own confusion.

Get Your Money for Nothing, and Your Change for Free. Create new things only as long as those new things deliver value. Be willing to swap them out for things that require equal effort. What in the beginning you thought you needed is never what is actually needed.

CHAPTER NINE

Change the World

Scrum has its origins in the world of software development. Now it's sweeping through myriad other places where work gets done. Diverse businesses are using it for everything from building rocket ships to managing payroll to expanding human resources, and it's also popping up in everything from finance to investment, from entertainment to journalism. I'm often amazed that a process I pioneered in 1993 to aid software development has proven itself universally applicable. Scrum accelerates human effort—it doesn't matter what that effort is.

In fact, I've begun to see it spring up in the most unlikely places, addressing the thorniest of humanity's problems. Think about some of those problems. For example, people living in poverty, which is not only demeaning but spawns a host of social ills, from crime and corruption to war and destruction. Then there's our system of education, which is failing students the world over. Instead of teaching twenty-first-century skills, we've mired our young people in ways of teaching and learning created in the nineteenth century. And the other out-of-whack element that comes to mind is government, which has seized up in many ways, predicating itself on ideas formed hundreds of years ago that no longer seem to fit with the way we live our lives.

It's easy to throw your hands up at the latest news of people dying in Africa, violence in our schools, or the endless posturing of people in power. It just seems like too much at times. But those problems, the hard problems, are precisely what Scrum is designed to address. In each of those cases people are now turning to Scrum to help solve those problems, and, just as in the business world, they're showing remarkable success.

Education

In some ways bedroom communities are the same the world over. Lying a few miles outside a major metropolis, they're where people move to buy a cheaper house, raise a family, and send their kids to school without many of the problems of the big city.

Alphen aan den Rijn is a pretty typical town in that sense. It lies in the west of the Netherlands, between Leiden and Utrecht, maybe forty-five minutes from Amsterdam. As you approach the town by road on a school day, all the traffic is headed in the other direction—to jobs elsewhere. Dairy farms and windmills, old and new, cover the countryside.

Inside the town the traffic is almost all bicycles. Hundreds and hundreds are headed to the local public secondary school, Ashram College. The school, like the town, is fairly typical for a Dutch school. There are about 1,800 students ranging in age from twelve to eighteen. Holland tracks its students early, splitting the children among: lower vocational programs, aimed at producing everything from hairdressers to mechanics to secretaries; higher vocational programs, aimed at gearing kids toward nursing, management, and engineering; and university-bound programs, aimed at those heading for medicine, the law, or research. The kids on the lower tracks can enter the workforce at sixteen, while those in the higher track might spend much of their twenties in university and professional education. Each of the different tracks requires some core classes in common, though each group is taught those subjects separately. Ashram teaches all three tracks. And one of those core subjects is what Willy Wijnands teaches to students at every grade level in the school: chemistry.

I'm sure you have memories of high school chemistry: lab tables in straight rows facing the teacher at the front of the room, perhaps a week of lecture followed by a few days working on a practical problem with a lab partner, the choice of whom was often strategic and much stressed over. Maybe you liked chemistry, maybe it bored you to tears, and maybe *Breaking Bad* gave you a new appreciation for the potential monetary reward of good lab technique and the importance of picking the right partner. Whatever your experience, once the teacher began talking about covalent bonds or some other abstruse concept, there was likely a near-audible *click* as you and your fellow students gazed out the window, doodled pictures, or thought about the cute boy or girl in the second row. Let's face it, in the American classroom, where chemistry leads, daydreaming often follows.

That's not what happens in Wijnands's classes, though. "See," he says as the students burst into the room and hurry to their desks—oddly, without sitting down. "I don't do anything." It's 8:30 a.m. on a normal Wednesday in September, and Wijnands's classroom does not look like one. None of the desks are in rows facing the front of the room. Instead, they're positioned so groups of four students can face one another.

Instead of sitting down at the beginning of class, these students pull out a large piece of paper covered with sticky notes, put it on the wall, and gather around. The paper is divided into a few large columns. *Alle items,* on the far left. Then *Te doen,* then *In uitvoering,* and finally, *Klaar.* As you might guess, they mean "All Items," "To do," "In Progress," and "Done."

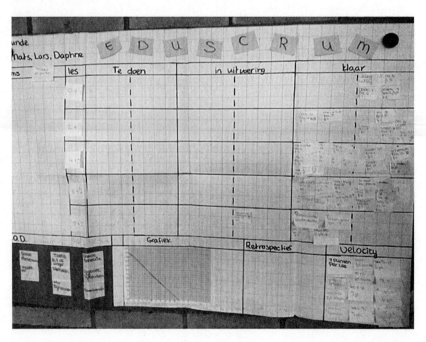

At the bottom of the columns are four additional headings: D.O.D, or Definition of Done; "Grafiek," which points to their Burndown Chart showing progress toward their goal; and, lastly, Retrospective and Velocity, where they measure how many "points" they accomplish during each lesson. Their Sprints are usually four or five weeks long, ending with a test.

In front of their Scrum boards—or "flops," as they call them in Dutch (a derivation of the word for "flip chart")—the students plot what lessons they're going to finish today. They move the sticky notes they think they can accomplish from the Backlog, *Alle items,* to *Te doen,* and get to work. Again, as Wijnands likes to say, he does nothing. The students open their books and start to teach themselves. Perhaps more important, they teach one another. Wijnands walks the room, looking at the Scrum boards and Burndown Charts. Occasionally, he'll spot a place where the students are having a problem, or he'll quickly explain a tricky concept, or he'll randomly take a story from the *Klaar* column and quiz each student on it, making sure all understand the concepts. If they don't, he moves it back to *Te doen.* Part of the Definition of Done, you see, is that everyone understands the material.

The students do have one part of the Scrum board that is unique to them: a "Definition of Fun." Not only does the work have to be complete, they also need to enjoy doing it. The three tests are Trust, Humor, and a uniquely Dutch word, *Gezelligheld.* There's no good English translation for it. It's described as "coziness," or "companionability," or "fun," or "pleasant," or seeing a friend after a long absence, or spending time with loved ones, or simply belonging. Actually, that strikes me as a perfect way to describe the feeling of support, enjoyment, hope, joy, comfort, and excitement of being on a really good team.

"You don't have to be the police," says Wijnands. "We now have another way to deal with managing students. They do everything. They even assign themselves homework!" Each team knows where they are in the material, the dates by which they have to accomplish interim steps, and if they'll need to do work outside of class to learn all the material in time. "They are self-organizing; they develop smarter and faster ways to study. One team started with the test and worked backward. A bunch of eleven-year-olds. 'Not good,' I told them. Their faces fell." Wijnands grins his contagious smile. "Then I said, 'Excellent!'"

Scrum, or eduScrum, as Wijnands calls his approach, is introduced to the students on the first day of class. The first thing they do is choose teams—cross-functional teams. Students rate themselves in various categories, everything from bravery to math enjoyment to taking account of others' feelings to "heading straight for the goal." Then the students are told to form teams that are cross-functional, that have all the skills needed to learn the material. This, says Wijnands, teaches them something just as important as the chemistry—it teaches them how to work with, and appreciate, people with different talents than their own.

Tim Jansen is seventeen years old. It's his senior year. He's now been doing Scrum for three years and is about to head to university, where he plans to study chemistry. He looks like your typical geek. "I am someone who can learn faster than others," he says. "But working together, you improve, you get better. I learn the material better by explaining it to others." He turns to Gudith Zwartz, who is sitting across the table from him. "She knows she can ask about content. I can ask *her* about organization. She can put it together better than I can."

Gudith looks quite different from Tim: slender, pretty, blond. "You get to know more about your classmates. You know who is good at which thing."

"Scrum helps the outsiders connect with the other parts of the class," chimes in her equally pretty and stylish friend Maneka Bowens. "Sometimes you choose the team, and sometimes you get chosen. You learn they are better than you at some qualities."

That kind of learning, says Wijnands, is part of the idea—to make unconscious skills conscious ones. Skills that can be tested on an exam are far from the only important ones. Helping students learn to identify and value different strengths in themselves and others is a twenty-first-century skill. That's something everyone needs to learn.

After they pick teams, the students are taught how to estimate not in hours or days, but in points. They then estimate each piece of the material they need to learn using the relative sizing inherent in the Fibonacci sequence by playing Planning Poker. Willy explains the idea of points quite simply. "Ignore all the measures you were told. There are no absolute measures. If I weigh fifty points," he says, pointing at a slender high school girl, "how many points do you weigh?"

"Um, forty?" She guesses.

"Why, thank you! I'd guess more around twenty, though."

At the end of each set of lessons, the teams do a Retrospective, asking themselves: "What went right?" "What could have gone better?" and "How can the team improve?"

This focus on teams, says Wijnands, is sometimes surprising to parents. He tells the story of one mother who called up and said that her daughter had done all the work. Why was she being forced to carry everyone else?

"I said the girl had to have the courage to tell others to do more. She did, and test scores went up. The mother called back to thank me. The students need to learn not only to work for themselves, but to work together."

The energy in the classrooms at Ashram is remarkable, and it translates into results. In the Dutch school system evaluative grades run from 1 to 10, and 5.5 is considered an acceptable passing grade. In Willy's classes a 7 is acceptable. And the students meet that baseline. Over the past year, says Wijnands, test scores have jumped more than 10 percent.

Willy learned about Scrum from his son-in-law, who works at a large technical company in the Netherlands that uses it. Willy's been a teacher for nearly four decades, and he says this is what he's been searching for the whole time: an approach that teaches children to teach themselves and to value their own skills and those of others. Also, to have fun while doing so.

An important thing to say about Scrum is that it rarely remains a one-off for long—it's built to *scale*. In the Netherlands schools, for example, eduScrum is not dependent on one person, even as great a teacher as Wijnands. While it may have started with Willy, and he may have convinced a few of his fellow chemistry teachers at Ashram to give it a try, it's now growing. Supported by the business community, there's now an eduScrum Foundation in the Netherlands that trains teachers and educates schools about Scrum. They've trained seventy-four teachers so far—in all subjects in twelve schools. They plan on growing by sixty teachers and fifteen schools a year. In five years, that will mean 300 more teachers and 75 more schools. A good start. I met with a few of the teachers from across the country, and they told me that this is the new Montessori. They see this as a *movement*.

It's not just happening in the Netherlands, though. In Arizona there's a charter school for poor, rural, Native American students that uses Scrum. In a few universities they are starting to teach it. At the Harvard Business School (HBS) they've built a new classroom called the "Innovation Lab," where all the instruction is based around teams. And as Professor Hirotaka Takeuchi of HBS told me, when you teach teams, the way to do it is Scrum.

While I was at Ashram, I spoke with some of the students there. When I asked what questions they had, one boy raised his hand.

"I can't believe you designed this for computer software," he said. "It seems perfectly designed for high school."

I felt tears in my eyes as I looked at this young man. I learned later he was autistic. Before Scrum he'd been unengaged and resigned. Scrum had given him a way to move forward, to actually enjoy school, and to become a better, more complete person.

Years ago, when I was trying to fix a few software companies, I hadn't realized that I was also creating something that could help fix people's lives. But it has. And perhaps nowhere more powerfully than in rural Uganda.

Poverty

Uganda is one of the poorest countries in the world. More than a third of the people there live on less than $1.25 a day. The vast majority of Ugandans reside in rural areas where poverty is endemic and people struggle to subsist by farming small family plots. Many of these places are beyond remote—days by foot from the nearest market town. Families have a hard time sending children to school, since their hands are needed to help on the farm. Girls especially drop out early. Life expectancy is fifty-three years. Infant mortality is more than 5 percent of live births, and about six thousand women die each year from complications in pregnancy. The life of a rural farmer in Uganda is not an easy one.

The Grameen Foundation grew out of the Nobel Prize–winner Muhammad Yunus's Grameen Bank, which pioneered microfinance for the extremely poor in Bangladesh. The Foundation focuses on helping lift the world's poor out of poverty, not by handouts but by harnessing the underappreciated strengths of the impoverished. In

Uganda they decided to try to do just that, by giving the poor the ability to share and build knowledge.

To do it, they recruited some 1,200 people in poor, rural areas—people they called "Community Knowledge Workers" (CKWs). The Foundation had already developed mobile applications for microfinance and payments, and they decided to give these knowledge workers not just banking information, but information they could use in their daily lives, which, in Uganda's case, meant it would be applied to farming. The Foundation provided access to the best agricultural practices by giving the workers smartphones and conveying the information that way.

Steve Bell, of the Lean Enterprise Institute and a Certified Scrum Master, recently visited two remote villages and described how it works. There's a meeting of farmers, standing up in a field. One farmer brought in a plant suffering from a disease. The CKWs quickly looked through pictures on the phone until they found a photo of a plant suffering from that particular disease. Then, instantly available was the scientific treatment for the disease—a treatment that didn't require expensive pesticides or chemicals, one that the farmer could immediately act on.

Bell says that fast transmission of actionable information would be powerful enough, but the app also links the farmers to others throughout Uganda. Using this connectivity, they can share precisely how much crops are selling for in the nearest market town, often days away. The farmers used to be at the mercy of middlemen who'd take advantage of the farmers' lack of market knowledge to set prices at whatever level they liked. Now farmers know how much the middlemen are making.

Bell told me the story of one woman who told him that the agricultural data alone doubled her yield. But the market data also doubled her prices. She used to get 300 shillings a bushel, but after she learned they were being sold for 1,000 shillings a bushel, she was able to negotiate a price of 600 shillings. Double the yield, double the profit, the same amount of work. That's what Scrum is designed to do, and that's how it delivered for her.

Eric Kamara heads the technology group for the Kinshasa office of the Grameen Foundation. His group uses Scrum to develop their applications. He says that each time a group asks for a feature set, his team rates it on a scale of 1 to 7 on three questions:

1. How important is this work to the mission of helping the poor?
2. How will this feature contribute to the work of the CKWs?
3. Is there partner support for the feature? (The Foundation prefers to work with partners such as the Gates Foundation rather than alone.)

This allows Kamara to prioritize the work using objective criteria. Before Scrum, he says, people were asking for everything at once. And with the limited resources of a nonprofit, they couldn't do everything, so the effect was doing nothing. Now in each Sprint the different groups who want features come in and pitch what they want done, and in a transparent way they see exactly how their feature stacks up against others. It helps a group with precious little to leverage determine what will have the greatest impact.

As I've seen elsewhere, this kind of work quickly spreads to the rest of the Kinshasa offices, changing the way they do their nine-to-five jobs. The office used to have the sort of weekly meeting that everyone dreads—an hours-long status update during which problems were stated and complained about, but little was done.

The meeting lasted forever, and everyone left unsatisfied. Often the only result was laying blame rather than seeking solutions. Now, Kamara says, every team has a Scrum board. Before the meeting, problems and blockages become easily apparent. These days the director of the office can simply walk around and instantly see where things are being blocked or stymied, just from checking out the state of the Scrum board.

If you talk to people in the world of nongovernmental organizations (NGOs), a common complaint is that their ranks are filled with people who share purpose and commitment but lack discipline. What Scrum can do is take people's passion and, by giving them clarity regarding what they should prioritize, harness it.

It's easy to make the *business* case for Scrum. If you use it, you'll make more money—a lot more. You'll get twice as much done in half the time. But the brightest promise for humanity lies with those people who've devoted their lives to helping the poorest of the poor. If Scrum can help these individuals who've been working on the margins to get the same effect, a giant step will have been made toward achieving a broad social good.

Not only will that "good" arrive sooner, it will also be measurable. Scrum gives people the ability to measure progress easily. At the Grameen Foundation they have what they call the "Progress Out of Poverty Index." It measures just how effective each program is. They can poll and *see* exactly the impact those Community Knowledge Workers with cell phones in rural villages are having. They can experiment with different ways of doing things. They can help people *innovate* their way out of poverty.

For me, it's amazing to see Scrum returning to its roots. When I first started Scrum, I was inspired by the Grameen Bank and other microfinance institutions and how they helped teams of poor people work together to leverage themselves out of poverty. They'd get together a team of them and have each person come up with a business plan laying out what they'd do with $25. One might want to buy a cart to sell fruit in the town square. Another might want to buy a sewing machine to make dresses she could sell. Only when all the loans on the team were paid back would the group be lent any more money. They'd meet each week to see how they could help one another. The results were amazing. Initially the woman with the sewing machine might make enough money to feed her children. A few weeks later she might be able to afford shoes for them. Then she could send them to school. A few cycles later she'd have a small business and could start building a real house. At the time, I told the software programmers I was working with: "These poor people have no shoes, and yet they can leverage their way out of poverty. *You* have shoes but no software. They've figured a way to work together to get out of misery. Are you willing to do the same?" And so Scrum was born.

Nonprofits are just one area where we can innovate social good. What about how we organize ourselves? What about government?

Government

Government is not only how we organize the public sphere—how we get roads and police and courts and the DMV—it's also how we formalize who we are as a people. It is a codification of who we believe we are. In the United States the fundamental aspirations of the American people are captured in a document signed by a bunch of rebels who surely would have been hanged separately if they didn't "hang" together—the Declaration of Independence. Penned by an aristocratic, idealistic, slaveholding landowner, the Declaration, surprisingly, captured a radical concept of what kind of people revolutionary era Americans wanted to be.

> We hold these truths to be self-evident, that all men are created equal, that they are endowed by their Creator with certain unalienable rights, that among these are Life, Liberty, and the pursuit of Happiness. That to secure these rights, Governments are instituted among Men, deriving their just powers from the consent of the governed.

It's hard to appreciate in the modern day what a departure from the norm those words represented. While the ideas of the Enlightenment had begun to spread, there were no democracies at the time. Rule was imposed from above, from the divine right of kings and the power of arms. Great empires ruled much of the world—not only Great Britain, but also France, Austria, Russia, and Ottoman. The idea that individuals were *endowed* with rights, rather than granted them by the powerful, was, to put it mildly, revolutionary.

The "republic" was a form of government that emerged from those ideals. Like Rodney Brooks's robot learning to walk, the United States lurched to its feet, stumbled, fell, and occasionally wandered down the wrong path. But those ideals inspired revolutions the world over, and today most major powers are governed, at least in form, by the people they purport to represent.

The problem, of course, is two-hundred-plus years of bureaucratic buildup—permanent interests embedded in the very structure of the government that make it hard for people's voices to be heard. Corruption—whether on the small scale of bureaucrats taking bribes for services, or on the grand scale of large banks garnering wealth by privatizing profit and socializing loss—is a result of a lack of transparency and the centralization of power in the hands of the few.

In most world capitals there has grown up a courtier class that constitutes the permanent government. Contracts are awarded, money is made, and power is conferred by "whom you know," not by "what you bring." Nowhere is this more evident than in the way politicians, generals, and powerful bureaucrats rotate from government to industry and back again. The number of four-star generals heading up defense contractors, or senators becoming lobbyists, or former administration officials heading up trade groups is staggering.

But as I emphasized in chapter three, it's pointless to look for evil people; look instead for evil systems. Let's ask a question that has a chance to actually change things: "What is the set of incentives that drives bad behavior?" I truly doubt that any of the Beltway bandits sees themselves as bad people, and I'd bet that most are truly well-meaning. It's the *system* that has failed them, and us. But how do we change it? How do we encourage transparency, priorities, and accountability? You know the answer: Scrum.

Let's start a few thousand miles west of Washington, D.C., in the Washington state capital, Olympia. There, the past two administrations—first a Republican, now a Democrat—have embraced what they call Lean government. The current governor, Jay Inslee, said in a campaign interview in the fall of 2012, "A lot of what the state does is make decisions. We want to find a way to leave less paper on a desk."[1]

The governor's plan has five points that could have been plucked from any campaign platform: 1. a "world-class" education system from preschool through college; 2. a "prosperous economy"; 3. making Washington a national leader in sustainable energy and a clean environment; 4. healthy and safe communities; 5. efficient, effective, and accountable government.

These are not revolutionary goals. This is what people *should* expect from their government. The very fact that they sound cliché is an indicator of their importance. A cliché, after all, is just a truth repeated enough times to become trite. But what's *different* about Inslee's administration is how they're going about it. They've dubbed their new approach SMART—Specific, Measureable, Attainable, Relevant, and Time-bound. In other words, they want to use Scrum. And, in fact, they are.

The office of the Chief Information Officer of the State of Washington is responsible not only for what technology is purchased, but how it's made. The CIO's office is made up of twenty people who are supposed to make sure massive IT failures, costing tens of millions of dollars, don't happen. Meanwhile, the department handles IT upgrades for the parts of the government that do everything from issue driver's licenses, to distribute unemployment benefits, to regulate fish and wildlife. In 2012 they oversaw eighty requests totaling more than $400 million. And they issue standards and guidance to various agencies on how to implement state policy.

To do that, they use Scrum. They've actually torn down the cubicle walls in their offices and formed into Scrum teams.

Michael DeAngelo, the Deputy CIO, says they try to deliver actionable, implementable policies to state departments every week: "We're updating our process for how our agencies submit plans for investment. We set the goal that every week we're going to change one thing. We're taking an incremental approach. We have a potentially shippable product every single week that can be felt by the agencies. They actually have something tangible." "Shippable product," in their case, means actionable changes to policy. It doesn't have to be a thing; it just has to be something, anything, that creates value.

Instead of trying to create a grand, overriding document anticipating every piece of the funding process, they've decided to do it piece by piece. They want to deliver improvements in how the state is run every single week.

Reaction, says DeAngelo, has been mixed. There's a huge fear of not having a perfect product. Speaking in August of 2013 he said: "Just last week we made a change to how customers call us. But there's a lot of documentation where we still have the old way listed—on our website, documents, that kind of thing. So there was all this other stuff we would have to change [first]. We decided not to wait, to just do it. We'll update documentation in the next Sprint. The alternative is that we don't give them a better way for months . . . we're robbing them of value."

The other thing the CIO's office is doing is trying to push Scrum through the entire state bureaucracy. It's why they've changed their own processes to Scrum—to become an example, to be able to speak from experience. The benefits are just too great not to.

But there are some roadblocks. DeAngelo says that one thing they've realized is that in some cases the Waterfall method is actually written into state law. Changing that can be tough. The State of Washington funds things in two-year cycles. "You have to ask for big chunks. You can't say we'll add value until you tell us to stop," says DeAngelo. "The government wants to see [that] it's going to cost this amount of money, [and that] we'll get this amount of value in this time frame. That's so they can talk about it with citizens. Even though we know it's much more inefficient."

Part of the problem is that in the United States, both at the federal and state level, legislatures are broken into committees. One group of lawmakers looks at education, another at crime, another at the budget, and yet another at social services.

"They are fractured. They never look at the whole picture," says Rick Anderson. He's a consultant to state agencies, counties, and cities in Washington, Oregon, California, and Hawaii. He has worked with the legislatures, and he says that while change may take a while, it has to happen.

He thinks they should start setting performance-based goals. "Okay, Agency X, here are your goals, here are your expected outcomes. Once you have that, you can start writing legislation that is outcome-based," he says.

In a revamped, Scrum-driven world, instead of approving a specific plan to build a bridge across a river, a legislative body would say to the highway department, "We want X number of people to be able to travel over this waterway in Y amount of time with Z cost. How you do that is up to you." That would allow for discovery and innovation.

Instead, the norm these days is construction projects that run hundreds of millions of dollars over budget. The reason? As crews work on the project, they discover new problems and new ways of solving them. Instead of stifling that kind of innovation with Change Control Boards and massive reporting, we should be encouraging it.

But what about those ideals that I started this section with— where a society shapes itself through a document? A constitution, say? Well, one country decided that the way to develop a constitution that truly represented the will of the people was to use Scrum.

In 2008 a completely avoidable financial crisis hit the world. Big banks spun prices out of control, leveraging themselves over and over again by taking on more bad debt than could ever be repaid. One of the countries hit hardest was Iceland. Privatized banks there had been spun off by the government and had taken huge risks in the financial markets. As they say on Wall Street, if you don't know who the sucker in the room is, you're the sucker. In this case, Iceland was the sucker. The amount of money they borrowed was staggering for such a small country. Eventually, the banks had valuations twelve times the size of the national budget. When it all came crashing down, the Icelandic "economic miracle" was in tatters.

In an expression of outrage, the citizens of Reykjavik took to the streets and banged pots and pans together outside the Althing, their parliament. The government that had overseen the financial practices collapsed in what became known as the "pots and pans revolution." The government stepped down, and new leadership promised a new constitution.

To write that constitution, some officials decided to be open and engage with the people. So they formed a constitutional committee, which decided to use Scrum. Each week the committee would meet, decide on one section of the document, and deliver it to the public every Thursday. Then they'd collect feedback from the people through Facebook and Twitter. In just a few months they had a new document that had won the overwhelming support of the Icelandic public. It was a new expression of how they saw themselves.

Unfortunately, the powers that had benefitted from the financial fraud struck back. After filing delay after delay—after obfuscating, complaining, and acting against the will of the people—a new parliament made up of the same parties that oversaw the destruction of Iceland's economy decided to simply ignore the new constitution. A key demand of the revolution was denied. For now, anyway.

The world is changing, and those who profit from secrecy and deception will soon find they have few places left to hide. Scrum is changing the world around them, and while they may fight a rearguard action, change is inevitable. The Scrum framework is just so much faster, transparent, and responsive to the wishes of the people that it will ultimately defeat the politicians who stand in its way.

Change or die.

How We'll All Work One Day

Earlier in this book I discussed the martial arts concept of *Shu Ha Ri*. People in the *Shu* state follow the rules exactly, so they learn the ideas behind them. People in the *Ha* state begin to create their own style within the rules, adapting them to their needs. People in the *Ri* state exist beyond the rules; they embody the ideals. Watching a true master in the *Ri* state is like looking at a moving work of art. His or her actions seem impossible, but that's because the master has become a philosophy in flesh, an idea made real.

All of which is to preface the fact that there *are* some rules in Scrum, and you would do well to both learn and transcend them. I've included them as an appendix to this book, "Implementing Scrum—How to Begin," and I've written chapter after chapter on why those rules exist, encouraging you, I hope, to apply them in your personal life, your company, and your community. The paradox of those rules, though, is that they eliminate boundaries, they create freedom—and for many, freedom can be terrifying.

One company that has learned how to set its employees free

and optimize innovation is Valve. To look at the firm is to behold how we all may inevitably organize ourselves, whether it's to make better software, raise people out of poverty, plan a wedding, or fix up a house.

Formed in the 1990s as a videogame company making revolutionary hits such as Half-Life and Portal, Valve is completely self-funded and owns all its own intellectual property. Almost all of its 300-plus employees are located in a single office tower in Bellevue, Washington. The company has over fifty million customers, and it makes hundreds of millions of dollars a year. And no one is really in charge.

Valve's origin is, of all places, Microsoft. Nowadays Microsoft is a very different company, but back in the 1990s it was the epitome of the top-down corporation. Everyone defined themselves by how far down the corporate pyramid they were from founder and CEO Bill Gates—back then the richest man in the world, and still one of the richest.

Greg Coomer is among the group of people who founded Valve. He worked for Gabe Newell, who headed a development group at Microsoft. Greg describes how that hyper-attentiveness to stature played out in the very tools people used: "At Microsoft there was an Outlook plug-in called 'Org Chart.' And any e-mail anyone would get, they'd click on that and see where the sender fit in the company. How many clicks away from Bill they were, how many direct reports they had, were they an enemy or a friend—all this could be discovered just from their position in the Org Chart."

Greg says that if you zoomed out, you could see that there was this giant pyramid with Bill at the top. If you zoomed in, there were bunches of smaller pyramids. "It was pyramids all the way down."

Except for Gabe Newell's group. There were a few hundred

people in it, and they all reported directly to him. "It stuck out visually in the 'Org Chart' app," says Greg. "It was something that didn't fit. And it was causing political problems, because he didn't have the right number of managers or the right structure." The company's response was almost like that of white blood cells massing to attack an infection. Now, of course, Microsoft already has three thousand people working on Scrum teams and is moving toward some twenty thousand people. But back then this "infection" had to be removed.

So Gabe, Greg, and a few others left and formed their own company, Valve. A few years ago Greg tried to compose an employee handbook explaining how Valve works. The document didn't list pay grades or whether glasses were covered by the flex spending account. Rather, it was an attempt to convey the Valve ethos.

"I figured out it was taking nine to sixteen months for people to internalize the Valve way of doing things. It took a long time for people to feel empowered," says Greg. The document was intended to ease people in quicker, but Greg and the other founders struggled with the words, because they didn't want it to seem that the explanation was coming from on high. The first section is "Welcome to Flatland":

> It's our shorthand way of saying that we don't have any management, and nobody "reports to" anybody else. We do have a founder/president, but even he isn't your manager. This company is yours to steer—toward opportunities and away from risks. You have the power to green-light projects. You have the power to ship products.
>
> A flat structure removes every organizational barrier between your work and the customer enjoying that work. Every

company will tell you that "the customer is boss," but here that statement has weight. There's no red tape stopping you from figuring out for yourself what our customers want, and then giving it to them.

If you're thinking to yourself, "Wow, that sounds like a lot of responsibility," you're right.[2]

Here's how a project starts at Valve. Someone decides to start it. That's it. They figure out what they think is the best use of their time and energy, what will serve the company and the customer the best, and they do it. How do they get other people to work with them on it? They convince them. If that other person thinks it's a good idea, they'll join that team, or "cabal," as it's called at Valve. All the hundreds of desks at Valve have wheels. As people start to work together on a project, they literally vote with their desks, moving them into a new configuration.

Greg describes the way it worked for a product called "Big Picture." One of Valve's biggest products is their Steam platform. It delivers videogames and software to users. Both Valve games and third-party games are on the platform. It's the dominant way PC games are delivered today. But as Greg recalls, at one point he and a couple of others feared they were already reaching as many customers as they could, more than fifty million.

"[We] started thinking about how our company was growing and how Steam is growing, and we were looking at what we thought would be the limit on the number of customers we could reach. We wanted to reach people in other places, in their living room, on mobile devices, whatever."

So he started talking to people—some designers, some other folks. He convinced them it was a good idea to come up with something that would work on televisions, phones, and tablets, and they created the idea of Big Picture—a way to deliver videogames to those platforms. But the people Greg had convinced didn't have all the skills needed to actually make it. They knew what they wanted it to look like, but they didn't have the ability to implement it.

"So we started mocking up what it could look like, and then we made a movie of how cool it would be. And we used that movie to recruit people to the project. We couldn't code it, [so] we needed to recruit people who could."

So they did. It shipped about a year later. Who decided when to ship it? The people who worked on it. Who decided it was good enough? The people who worked on it.

"When a company has optimized itself around innovation, they usually change in a fundamental way by eliminating internal structures and hierarchies, any internal structure," says Greg. Valve operates that way all the time. They don't wait to be forced into change by a crisis; they are *constantly* changing. It's the day-to-day way they run the company. From the *Valve Handbook*:

Valve is not averse to all organizational structure—it crops up in many forms all the time, temporarily. But problems show up when hierarchy or codified divisions of labor either haven't been created by the group's members or when those structures persist for long periods of time. We believe those structures inevitably begin to serve their own needs rather than those of Valve's customers. The hierarchy will begin to reinforce its own structure by hiring people who fit its shape, adding people to fill subordinate support roles. Its members are also incented to engage in rent-seeking behaviors that take advantage of the power structure rather than focusing on simply delivering value to customers.[3]

It may seem that Valve would be vulnerable to freeloaders—to people who want to take advantage of the system—but peer review is constant. Sure, people get to decide what to work on, but if they can't convince anyone else it's a good idea, maybe it really isn't. Greg says that instead of having the *luxury* of having someone tell you what to do, you have a group of peers telling you what they think of what you've decided to do.

It isn't a perfect system. No human organization is. But usually at Valve, personnel concerns are raised first by fellow team members talking with one another. They may bring in others to consult. It may result in feedback, a harsh corrective move, or even dismissal. But it's a team decision.

The exception occurred in 2013, when Valve developed a problem their system wasn't quite able to handle. For the first time ever they hired a large group of people all at once. They had decided to branch into hardware and mobile, and they simply didn't have the skills to do it. So they hired a bunch of people to tackle the problem.

But hiring that many people simultaneously who weren't acclimated to the Valve way of doing things caused problems. There were pockets of workers not making decisions in the traditional Valve way. *They were telling other people what to do.* And, most damning, not performing up to the high Valve standards. Normally, other team members wouldn't tolerate that kind of behavior, but because everyone in the group was new, their peers didn't have enough confidence in the Valve way to take action.

"So a group of the core Valve people who have been around

for a while took action to protect the Valve ethos. Even though they had to act *outside* of the ethos to do it," says Greg. The company fired a few dozen people at once. Talking to Greg, you can tell he sees that as a failure. He describes it as an almost biological reaction, one that was oddly parallel to how Microsoft acted toward Valve's founders: organisms attacking foreign invaders to protect the whole.

"We've been talking a lot about what it means to our stated goals that we had to act outside them," reflects Greg. "And how we can avoid it in the future. And not have to rely on a group of people who have been at the company a long time." He stops for a moment and then says with confidence, "By this time next year we'll have figured it out."

There's a faith in what they've done. They've consistently sought to maximize human freedom, ability, and creativity. While there have been occasional hiccups, it's just too powerful a way of operating not to be replicated over and over again.

"This is a capitalist innovation as powerful as many industrial innovations that changed the nature of work," he says. "It is so useful and so successful that there is no way it can't be a force of change in the world."

Do they use Scrum? Well, says Greg, you walk down the hallway, and you see a lot of whiteboards on wheels covered with sticky notes. But they don't *force* people to use it; they let people decide what process is right for them. As with most matters, Greg and the other founders refrain from telling anyone what to do. But a lot of Valve's workers have decided that, given the choice to do anything, they choose Scrum. And that's enough for me.

You don't see many companies like Valve yet. But more are appearing each day. And not only in software. Morning Star, the global leader in tomato processing, has no bosses. Each employee negotiates with other employees as to roles and responsibilities, whether they involve sales, driving trucks, or doing sophisticated engineering. With any company, first you have to get employees to set themselves free, and then you have to get them to accept the responsibility that comes with that.

Or, as Funkadelic put it back in 1970, "Free your mind . . . and your ass will follow."

What Can't We Do?

Cynicism is perhaps a rational response to despair, but it is one of the most corrosive of human states. The early years of this century have been rife with the elements that breed cynicism: senseless wars draped in patriotism, nihilistic terrorism masquerading as faith, greed cloaked in ideological righteousness, ambitious political courtiers pursuing their own selfish ends.

The cynic will sigh knowingly and say, "That's just the way the world works. Humans are essentially corrupt and selfish— pretending otherwise is just naive." In that way they justify constraints and rationalizes limits.

Over the past two decades I've delved deeply into the literature of what makes greatness. The surprising answer is that, fundamentally, humans *want* to be great. People want to do something purposeful—to make the world, even if just in a small way, a better place. The key is getting rid of what stands in their way, removing the impediments to their becoming who they're capable of becoming.

That's what Scrum does. It sets goals and systematically, step by step, works out how to get there. And even more important, it identifies what is stopping us from getting there.

Scrum is the code of the anti-cynic. Scrum is not wishing for a better world, or surrendering to the one that exists. Rather, it is a practical, actionable way to implement change. I know of Scrum projects aimed at delivering vaccines to endangered children, and of others intended to build houses more cheaply, eliminate petty corruption, catch violent criminals, eliminate hunger, and send people to other planets.

None of the above are dreamy desires—rather, they're actionable plans. Make no mistake, these plans will have to be inspected, adapted, and changed every step of the way, but they're in *motion*. All around the world, rapid iterations are occurring, propelling us toward a better world.

That's what I hope you'll take away from this book: the knowledge that it is possible—that you can change things, that you don't have to accept the way things are.

All men dream: but not equally. Those who dream by night in the dusty recesses of their minds wake in the day to find that it was vanity: but the dreamers of the day are dangerous men, for they may act their dreams with open eyes, to make it possible.

—T. E. Lawrence, *Seven Pillars of Wisdom*[4]

Don't listen to cynics who tell you what can't be done. Amaze them with what can.

THE TAKEAWAY

Scrum Accelerates All Human Endeavors. The type of project or problem doesn't matter—Scrum can be used in any endeavor to improve performance and results.

Scrum for Schools. In the Netherlands, a growing number of teachers are using Scrum to teach high school. They see an almost immediate improvement in test scores of more than 10 percent. And they're engaging all sorts of students, from vocational to gifted.

Scrum for Poverty. In Uganda, the Grameen Foundation is using Scrum to deliver agricultural and market data to poor rural farmers. The result: double the yield and double the revenue for some of the poorest people on the planet.

Rip Up Your Business Cards. Get rid of all titles, all managers, all structures. Give people the freedom to do what they think best and the responsibility to be accountable for it. You'll be surprised at the results.

ACKNOWLEDGMENTS

Any project isn't the result of one person's work; it is the product of a team, and this book is no exception.

First I'd like to thank my son, J. J. Sutherland. He suggested we write a book together on the truly remarkable journey Scrum has taken me on a few years ago. He wanted a break from a decade of running from one war and disaster to another for NPR, and he thought the story of how Scrum came to be, why it works, and how it has changed the world not only was an important one to tell but would also be a lot of fun. The book you hold, while my story, is the product of many hours together, but he is the one who put the words on the page.

Howard Yoon, the savviest of literary agents, asked us to think bigger and broader and farther. His insight, advice, wisdom, and just plain canny know-how not only made this book happen but took it to a vastly different scale.

It's not often you get the chance to work with a true master of his craft, and I've been incredibly lucky to have the chance with Rick Horgan at the Crown Publishing Group. His deft and thorough touch just makes stuff *better*. And he makes it look so *easy*. Hats off, and true thanks.

Chief Product Owner Alex Brown, Joe Justice, and the rest

of the team at Scrum, Inc., shared critical ideas, boundless energy, and deep experience.

I'd also like to thank:

Professors Hirotaka Takeuchi and Ikujiro Nonaka, whose work sparked the idea of Scrum and who have since become good friends.

My fellow co-creator, Ken Schwaber, whose irascible dogged-ness helped shape Scrum and make it the force that it is today.

Most of all, my wife, Arline. She was there from the beginning and, as a Unitarian-Universalist minister, introduced Scrum to many churches. She made the world a better place when she showed us how to Scrum an entire organization.

And finally, I'd like to thank the hundreds of thousands of Scrum Masters and Product Owners and Teams across the planet who actually live Scrum every day. You make Scrum the vibrant and positive force that it is in the world, and you never cease to astound me with what you have accomplished with it.

IMPLEMENTING SCRUM — HOW TO BEGIN

Now that you've read the book, here's how to start a Scrum project in a nutshell. This is a very broad stroke description of the process, but it should be enough to get you started. The book was written to give you the *why* behind Scrum. This will, in an abbreviated form, give you the *how*.

1. Pick a **Product Owner.** This person is the one with the vision of what you are going to do, make, or accomplish. They take into account risks and rewards, what is possible, what can be done, and what they are passionate about. (See *Chapter Eight:* **Priorities** for more.)

2. Pick a **Team.** Who will be the people actually doing the work? This team needs to have all the skills needed to take the Product Owners' vision and make it a reality. Teams should be small, 3 to 9 people is the rule of thumb. (See *Chapter Three:* **Teams** for more.)

3. Pick a **Scrum Master.** This is the person who will coach the rest of the team through the Scrum framework, and help the team eliminate anything that is slowing them down. (See *Chapter Four:* **Waste** for more.)

4. Create and prioritize a **Product Backlog.** This is a list at a high level of everything that needs to be built or done to make that vision a reality. This backlog exists and evolves over the lifetime of the product; it is the product road map. At any point, the Product Backlog is the single, definitive view of "everything that could be done by the team ever, in order of priority." Only a single Product Backlog exists; this means the Product Owner is required to make prioritization decisions across the entire spectrum. The Product Owner should consult with all stakeholders and the team to make sure they are representing both what people want and what can be built. (See *Chapter Eight:* **Priorities** for more.)

5. Refine and Estimate the **Product Backlog.** It is crucial that the people who are actually going to complete the items in the Product Backlog estimate how much effort they will take. The team should look at each Backlog item, and see if it is actually doable. Is there enough information to complete the item? Is it small enough to estimate? Is there a Definition of Done, that is, everyone agrees on what standards must be met to call something "done"? Does it create visible value? Each item must be able to be shown, to be demonstrated, hopefully to be potentially shippable. Do not estimate the Backlog in hours, because people are absolutely terrible at that. Estimate by relative size: Small, Medium, or Large. Or even better use the Fibonacci sequence and estimate the point value for each item: 1, 2, 3, 5, 8, 13, 21, etc. (See *Chapter Six:* **Plan Reality, Not Fantasy** for more.)

6. **Sprint Planning.** This is the first of the Scrum meetings. The team, the Scrum Master, and the Product Owner sit down to plan the Sprint. Sprints are always a fixed length of time that is less than a month. Most people now run one- or two-week

Sprints. The team looks at the top of the Backlog and forecasts how much of it they can complete in this Sprint. If the team has been going for a few Sprints, they should take in the number of points they did in the last Sprint. That number is known as the team's **Velocity.** The Scrum Master and the team should be trying to increase that number every Sprint. This is another chance for the team and the Product Owner to make sure that everyone understands exactly how these items are going to fulfill the vision. Also during this meeting everyone should agree on a Sprint Goal, what everyone wants to accomplish with this Sprint.

One of the pillars of Scrum is that once the team has committed to what they think they can finish in one Sprint, that's it. It cannot be changed, it cannot be added to. The team must be able to work autonomously throughout the Sprint to complete what they forecast they could. (See *Chapter Four:* **Time** and *Chapter Six:* **Plan Reality, Not Fantasy** for more.)

7. **Make Work Visible.** The most common way to do this in Scrum is to create a **Scrum Board** with three columns: To Do, Doing, Done. Sticky notes represent the items to be completed and the team moves them across the Scrum board as they are completed, one by one.

Another way to make work visible is to create a **Burndown Chart.** On one axis is the number of points the team has taken into the Sprint, on the other is the number of days. Every day the Scrum Master tallies up the number of points completed and graphs them on the Burndown chart. Ideally there will be a steep downward slope leading to zero points left on the last day of the Sprint. (See *Chapter Seven:* **Happiness** for more.)

8. **Daily Stand-up** or **Daily Scrum.** This is the heartbeat of

Scrum. Each day, at the same time, for no more than fifteen minutes, the team and the Scrum Master meet and answer three questions:

- What did you do yesterday to help the team finish the Sprint?
- What will you do today to help the team finish the Sprint?
- Is there any obstacle blocking you or the team from achieving the Sprint Goal?

That's it. That's the whole meeting. If it takes more than fifteen minutes, you're doing it wrong. What this does is help the whole team know exactly where everything is in the Sprint. Are all the tasks going to be completed on time? Are there opportunities to help other team members overcome obstacles? There's no assigning of tasks from above—the team is autonomous; *they* do that. There's no detailed reporting to management. The Scrum Master is responsible for making the obstacles to the team's progress, or impediments, go away. (See *Chapter Four:* **Time** and *Chapter Six:* **Plan Reality, Not Fantasy** for more.)

9. **Sprint Review** or **Sprint Demo.** This is the meeting where the team shows what they have accomplished during the Sprint. Anyone can come, not only the Product Owner, the Scrum Master, and the team, but stakeholders, management, customers, whoever. This is an open meeting where the team demonstrates what they were able to move to Done during the Sprint.

The team should only demo what meets the Definition of Done. What is totally and completely finished and can be delivered without any more work. It may not be a completed product, but it should be a completed feature of one. (See *Chapter Four:* **Time** for more.)

10. **Sprint Retrospective.** After the team has shown what they've accomplished during the last Sprint—that thing that is "done" and can potentially be shipped to customers for feedback—they sit down and think about what went right, what could have gone better, and what can be made better in the next Sprint. What is the improvement in the process that they, as a team, can implement right away?

    To be effective, this meeting requires a certain amount of emotional maturity and an atmosphere of trust. The key thing to remember is that you're not seeking someone to blame; you're looking at the process. Why did that happen that way? Why did we miss that? What could make us faster? It is crucial that people as a team take responsibility for their process and outcomes, and seek solutions as a team. At the same time, people have to have the fortitude to bring up the issues that are really bothering them in a way that is solution oriented rather than accusatory. And the rest of the team has to have the maturity to hear the feedback, take it in, and look for a solution rather than getting defensive.

    By the end of the meeting the team and the Scrum Master should agree on one process improvement that they will implement in the next Sprint. That process improvement, sometimes called the *kaizen,* should be put into the next Sprint's backlog, with acceptance tests. That way the team can easily see if they actually implemented the improvement, and what effect it had on velocity. (See *Chapter Seven:* **Happiness** for more.)

11. Immediately start the next Sprint cycle, taking the Team's experience with impediments and process improvements into account.

NOTES

CHAPTER ONE

1. Eggen, Dan, and Griff Witte. "The FBI's Upgrade That Wasn't; $170 Million Bought an Unusable Computer System." *Washington Post,* August 18, 2006: A1.

2. *Status of the Federal Bureau of Investigation's Implementation of the Sentinel Project.* US Department of Justice, Office of the Inspector General. Report 11-01, October 2010.

3. Ibid.

4. Ohno, Taiichi. *Toyota Production System: Beyond Large-scale Production* (Cambridge, MA: Productivity, 1988).

5. Roosevelt, Theodore. "Citizenship in a Republic." Speech at the Sorbonne, Paris, France, April 23, 1910.

CHAPTER TWO

1. Takeuchi, Hirotaka, and Ikujiro Nonaka. "The New New Product Development Game." *Harvard Business Review,* Jan./Feb. 1986: 285–305.

2. Schwaber, Ken. "Scrum Development Process," in *OOPSLA Business Object Design and Implementation Workshop,* J. Sutherland, D. Patel, C. Casanave, J. Miller, and G. Hollowell, eds. (London: Springer, 1997).

3. Deming, W. Edwards. "To Management." Speech at Mt. Hakone Conference Center, Japan, 1950.

CHAPTER THREE

1. Takeuchi, Hirotaka, and Ikujiro Nonaka. "The New New Product Development Game." *Harvard Business Review* (Jan./Feb. 1986): 285–305.

2. MacArthur, Douglas. "The Long Gray Line." Speech at West Point, New York, 1962.

3. Ibid.

4. Feynman, Richard. *Report of the Presidential Commission on the Space Shuttle Challenger Accident,* Appendix F—Personal Observations on Reliability of Shuttle. Report (1986).

5. Warrick, Joby, and Robin Wright. "U.S. Teams Weaken Insurgency in Iraq." *Washington Post,* September 6, 2006.

6. Flynn, Michael, Rich Jergens, and Thomas Cantrell. "Employing ISR: SOF Best Practices." *Joint Force Quarterly* 50 (3rd Quarter 2008): 60.

7. Lamb, Christopher, and Evan Munsing. "Secret Weapon: High-value Target Teams as an Organizational Innovation." Institute for National Strategic Studies: Strategic Perspectives, no. 4, 2011.

8. Brooks, Frederick P. *The Mythical Man-Month: Essays on Software Engineering* (Reading, MA: Addison-Wesley, 1975).

9. Cowan, Nelson. "The Magical Number 4 in Short-Term Memory: A Reconsideration of Mental Storage Capacity." *Behavioral and Brain Sciences* 24 (2001): 87–185.

10. Nisbett, Richard, Craig Caputo, Patricia Legant, and Leanne Marecek. "Behavior as Seen by the Actor and as Seen by the Observer." *Journal of Personality and Social Psychology* 27.2 (1973): 154–64.

11. Milgram, Stanley. "The Perils of Obedience." *Harper's Magazine,* 1974.

CHAPTER FOUR

1. Marvell, Andrew. "To His Coy Mistress," (1681).

CHAPTER FIVE

1. Ohno, Taiichi. *Toyota Production System: Beyond Large-scale Production* (Cambridge, MA: Productivity, 1988).

2. Strayer, David, Frank Drews, and Dennis Crouch. "A Comparison of the Cell Phone Driver and the Drunk Driver." *Human Factors* 48.2 (Summer 2006): 381–91.

3. Sanbonmatsu, D. M., D. L. Strayer, N. Medeiros-Ward, and J. M. Watson. "Who Multi-Tasks and Why? Multi-Tasking Ability, Perceived Multi-Tasking Ability, Impulsivity, and Sensation Seeking." *PLoS ONE* (2013) 8(1): e54402. doi:10.1371/journal.pone.0054402.

4. Weinberg, Gerald M. *Quality Software Management* (New York: Dorset House, 1991).

5. Pashler, Harold. "Dual-task Interference in Simple Tasks: Data and Theory." *Psychological Bulletin* 116.2 (1994): 220–44.

6. Charron, Sylvain, and Etienne Koechlin. "Divided Representation of Concurrent Goals in the Human Frontal Lobes." *Science* 328.5976 (2010): 360–63.

7. Wilson, Glenn. The Infomania Study. Issue brief, http://www.drglennwilson.com/Infomania_experiment_for_HP.doc.

8. Womack, James P., Daniel T. Jones, and Daniel Roos. *The Machine That Changed the World: The Story of Lean Production* (New York: HarperPerennial, 1991).

9. Avnaim-Pesso, Liora, Shai Danziger, and Jonathan Levav. "Extraneous Factors in Judicial Decisions." *Proceedings of the National Academy of Sciences of the United States of America.* 108.17 (2011).

10. Vohs, K., R. Baumeister, J. Twenge, B. Schmeichel, D. Tice, and J. Crocker.

Decision Fatigue Exhausts Self-Regulatory Resources—But So Does Accommodating to Unchosen Alternatives (2005).

CHAPTER SIX

1. Cohn, Mike. *Agile Estimation and Planning* (Upper Saddle River, NJ: Prentice Hall, 2005).

2. Bikhchandani, Sushil, David Hirshleifer, and Ivo Welch. "A Theory of Fads, Fashion, Custom, and Cultural Change as Informational Cascades." *Journal of Political Economy* 100.5 (1992): 992–1026.

3. Thorndike, Edward Lee. "A Constant Error in Psychological Ratings." *Journal of Applied Psychology* 4.1 (1920): 25–29.

4. Dalkey, Norman, and Olaf Helmer. "An Experimental Application of the Delphi Method to the Use of Experts." *Management Science* 9.3 (Apr. 1963): 458–67.

CHAPTER SEVEN

1. Lyubomirsky, Sonja, Laura King, and Ed Diener. "The Benefits of Frequent Positive Affect: Does Happiness Lead to Success?" *Psychological Bulletin* 131.6 (2005): 803–55.

2. Spreitzer, Gretchen, and Christine Porath. "Creating Sustainable Performance." *Harvard Business Review* (Jan–Feb 2012): 3–9.

3. Ibid.

4. The Fool, *King Lear,* act 1, scene 4.

CHAPTER EIGHT

1. Shook, John. "The Remarkable Chief Engineer." Lean Enterprise Institute, February 3, 2009.

2. Ford, Daniel. *A Vision So Noble: John Boyd, the OODA Loop, and America's War on Terror* (CreateSpace Independent, 2010).

3. Boyd, John. *New Conception.* 1976.

4. Ibid.

CHAPTER NINE

1. Shannon, Brad. "McKenna, Inslee Outline Plans to Bring Efficiency to Government." *The Olympian,* October 6, 2012.

2. *Valve Handbook for New Employees* (Bellevue, WA: Valve Press, 2012).

3. Ibid.

4. Lawrence, T. E. *Seven Pillars of Wisdom: A Triumph* (London: Cape, 1973).

INDEX